# THE CHRISTIAN DREAMS, VISIONS, AND PROPHECY

❖ ❖ ❖ ❖ ❖ ❖ ❖ ❖ ❖ ❖ ❖ ❖ ❖ ❖ ❖ ❖ ❖ ❖ ❖

*Robert Grey*

Order this book online at www.trafford.com
or email orders@trafford.com

Most Trafford titles are also available at major online book retailers.

Illustrated by Robert Grey

Note for Librarians: A cataloguing record for this book is available from Library
and Archives Canada at www.collectionscanada.ca/amicus/index-e.html

Printed in Victoria, BC, Canada.

ISBN: 978-1-4251-8267-0

We at Trafford believe that it is the responsibility of us all, as both individuals
and corporations, to make choices that are environmentally and socially sound.
You, in turn, are supporting this responsible conduct each time you purchase a
Trafford book, or make use of our publishing services. To find out how you are
helping, please visit www.trafford.com/responsiblepublishing.html

Our mission is to efficiently provide the world's finest, most comprehensive
book publishing service, enabling every author to experience success.
To find out how to publish your book, your way, and have it available
worldwide, visit us online at www.trafford.com

Last Revised: 3/17/2010

 www.trafford.com

North America & International
toll-free: 1 888 232 4444 (USA & Canada)
phone: 250 383 6864 ♦ fax: 812 355 4082

# ABOUT THE AUTHOR

A pentecostal preacher who lived and preach the gospel of Christ over these forty plus years, a man with many years of experiences regarding the revelations of the Lord

You may be very surprise to know that the very thing the Lord reveal to the apostles he reveal the same thing to me too, such as the soul of man, the rapture, Jesus as bright as the sun, a vision of the apostle Paul, also the fall of Russia, just to name a few.

This is not a dream book, this is a man who God gave insight through dreams, visions, and prophecy.

## WHAT'S IN A DREAM

*D*reams are giving us a glimpse into the future beyond our natural ability. There are thousands of people all over the world that can testify that God talk to them through a dream or a vision. Still some people choose to go on doubting this true and loving divine intelligence that is constantly trying to guide us into a higher level that we know not of. I know a young man who was looking for a job some years ago) he told me that he had a dream seeing a little girl who he never saw before and the little girl had a small knife in her hand.

He said when he woke from the dream he did not know what to make of it because he did not understand the dream. So he went to look for a job and saw the same little girl with the same little knife in her hand at the place where he got the job. Dreams are taking us into a world all unknown to the human intelligence.

God deals with the spirit of men and women while we sleep. Listen to what Job have to say. For God speaketh once, yea twice, yet man perceiveth it not. In a dream, in a vision of the night, when deep sleep falleth upon men, in slumberings upon his bed. Then he openeth the ears of men, and sealeth their instruction. That he may withdraw man from his purpose, and hide pride from man. He keepeth back his soul from the pit, and his life from perishing by the sword Job 33: 14-18. Man cannot argue with what God put in his own power. Are All the laws of nature understood? I doubt it. New discoveries are found all the time. Man need to appreciate dreams for the insight they are giving to us. There are many people who had dreams but do not understand what they dream, so I hope my experience will give you a better understanding of your dreams.

God is talking to man all the time but the devil do not want you to understand that God is really talking to you so he confuse the mind of many so that they cannot pay attention to God when He speak, they would rather believe anything else than to believe that God is talking to them, isn't that strange?

✧ ✧ ✧ ✧ ✧ ✧ ✧ ✧ ✧ ✧ ✧ ✧ ✧ ✧ ✧ ✧ ✧ ✧ ✧

# THE BOOK OF REVELATION

*I*N GR, it is Apocalypsis, MEANING unveiling, some times called the Apocalypse, it is the last book of the Bible and the only book of the new testament that is exclusively prophetic in character. It belong to the group of prophetic writings in which the divine message is conveyed by dreams and visions. The title of which the book itself assumes Rev 1:v1 may mean either "the Revelation which Christ possesses and imparts, or the unveiling of Christ himself. Grammatically, the unveiling of Christ himself is preferable, because this text states that God gave this disclosure to Christ that he might impart it to his servants.

Revelation was assign to John, who was well known among the churches of Asia minor. He was also a brother who also suffer persecution, and was called and was given visions of a prophet and the Lord send his angel to let John know the importance of the revelation. It is impossible to use a short moment to go into evidence to prove that the Bible is divine Revelation, it is not enough to speak of the faithful church down through the centuries "the Bible is the word of God, and that it is the only infallible rule of faith and practice. And that Christ and his apostles believed and taught that the Bible in its intirety is divine Revelation and is brought out by many great writers with overwhelming evidence. For example, Jesus said, the scripture cannot be broken (John 10:35) and the Apostle Paul said, All scripture is given by inspiration of God, 2 Tim 3:16 Peter declares, knowing this first, that no prophecy of the scripture is of any private interpretation. For the prophecy came not in old time by the will of man, but holy men of God spoke as they were moved by the Holy Ghost. 2 Peter 1:20-21.

As for the writers of the new testament, what the scripture says, God says. The scripture cannot be broken. The old testament is fulfilled in the new testament, and the writers of the new testament claimed an equal authority. See,for example, 2 Thess'3:6,14-16, Peter said Paul epistles are scripture (2 Peter 3:15-16) and Paul quotes a saying of Jesus found in matt 10:10 and Luke 10:7, as scripture (1 Tim 5:8). On the nature of the Bible as Revelation, the reader are invited to meditate on the word of God. Jesus said men shall not live by bread alone, but by every word that proceedeth out of the mouth of God, Matt 4:v4. Peter refers to the prophetic word as "more sure" than his own eye witness experience of the transfiguration 2 Peter 1:16-19, and he says to this word, you do well to devote yourselves, as to a light shining in a dark place. It is very important for God's people to keep the world and its pleasures out of their lives so he can show us great and mighty things that we know not of when we call upon him. Jer 33:3.

✧ ✧ ✧ ✧ ✧ ✧ ✧ ✧ ✧ ✧ ✧ ✧ ✧ ✧ ✧ ✧ ✧ ✧

# REVELATION

*D*reams, visions, and prophecy, are revelations. The word revelation is derived from Latin, and means "unveiling." It is the translation of the Greek apokalypsis, meaning to unveil, reveal,and uncover, or the lifting up of a curtain so that all may see what was previously veiled. The revelation of the Lord is simply the unveiling of facts and truths which man could not possible know of on his own, but which are divinely revealed by the spirit of God. About one fifth of the Bible is prophecy which requires a revelation, and these revelations comes through dreams, visions, and prophecy.

Then there are many other parts of the Bible such as creation, Lucifer's reign, God's plan, and many other things that had to be revealed before man could possible know the facts about them. Man's intellectual and moral nature requires a revelation from God. Such revelation will help man to preserve and insure the moral and spiritual progress that man needs to achieve and a higher nature that he cannot hope to reach on his own. It is within man's moral makeup an intuition, a reason, and a hunger for the supernatural and to know things unrevealed.

These natural cravings must be satisfied-The only way these natural desires of man can be met is by the means of a supernatural revelation, only a revelation beyond the human ability can bring them to us. And yet when they comes to us through a dream, or a vision, or prophecy, and although they fulfill JOEL 2:28-29, still there are religious leaders who say they are Christians and yet they cannot believe that which was spoken by the prophet Joel that God's people will dream, dreams, and see visions, and that we will prophesy. This is outrageous, and leads me to ask this question, how do these people expect God to give us his revelation? or what do they want God to say or do in order for them to believe.

If they want God to give us his revelation according to their theological training and educational ability they have a long time to wait. Many of God's people are sitting under the leadership of these leaders, but God have a way to pass them by and raise up people with no theological training or educational ability and anoint them with the Holy Ghost and fire so he can get the glory that due to his holy name, believe the word of God and you will do well. God have no interest in man's intellectual ability because it is foolishness where God is concern. God have the ability to teach us far above, above any human educator. God will call the unlearned and anoint them with the Holy Ghost and fire and put to shame the wise, 1 Cor 1: 25-29.

# INTRODUCTION

*W*hat are dreams? dreams are forerunners of informations comes to inform us or forewarn us of what our senses and ability are not aware of, and also of future events. Some dreams can be surprisingly accurate so God's people are encourage to give much attention to dreams because the Lord could be talking to you. Some times the Lord will talk to us in a dream and tell us what to do or what not to do, at other times he give us a scripture so we can go and read it. When Jesus was born and Herod seek the young child life to destroy him an angel of the Lord talk to Joseph in a dream to take the young child and his mother and flee into EGYPT and stay there until I bring you words, Matt 2:13-15).

Some times we will have, dreams that we do not understand so it is wise to go to the scripture for the understanding because some dreams are according to the scripture but they comes in the form of an illustration or a picture, meaning that what you dream represent something. For example, a lion and a flock of goats, the lion is the devil and the goats represent the people, the vision is talked about in the book.

## A VISION OF A DEAD WOMAN OPEN HER EYES, WHAT COULD THIS MEAN?

$\mathcal{O}$ne night I dream that my big sister was dead and her daughter took me into the house where she was lying in a box, she was covered from head to toe, so her daughter remove the covering from her face, her eyes was closed, I called her and said, hi sis, and the dead woman open her eyes and looked at me, her daughter saw it also. In the dream I told some people that was in the house about what happen but they did not believe me. About 30 days after this dream her daughter called me and said her mother was sick and in the hospital. When I heard that I know that my sister was going to die, but I could not tell her because I did not want to frighten her. But thank God she was a child of God for many years. And she died two months after the dream.

What is the meaning of a dead woman to open her eyes? the interpretation of the dream is found in John ll:25-26, and Jesus said unto her, I am the resurrection and the life, he that believeth in me, though he were dead, yet shall he live. And whosoever liveth and believeth in me shall never die, believest thou this?

The Lord want me to know that although my sister was dead she is still alive.

## A SPIRITUAL INTERPRETATION

$\mathcal{O}$ne night in 2006 I had a vision of a very long bridge about 1/2 a mile long with only two pillars, one pillar at each end of the bridge, nothing in the middle and very high. ON top of one of the pillar was one bluish looking eye like unto the eye of a man looking down at me, I became very angry and went to the pillar with the eye and shook it very hard, and the bridge broke in two pieces and fell to the ground (The interpretation) the eye is the devil watching me, and the crumbling of the bridge means the plan of the devil for me crumbled. This vision represent victory, the Lord want me to know that I am winning. IF you are defeated in a dream, you must be very careful because it could happen to you in real life because dreams are illustrations or a picture of what will be, they are telling us very important things.

## THE CHRISTIAN DREAMS, VISIONS, AND PROPHECY

Some people believe that a dream is when you are sleeping and a vision is when you are not sleeping but according to Bible dictionary, it explain that it is impossible to draw a sharp line of demarcation between a dream and a vision, that's how close they are. In the early times of the patriarchs God often appeared to godly men but from the time of Jacob and onward his revelations were more often in dreams.(contrast for instance of the experience of Abraham in Genesis 18: with that of Jacob in Genesis 28: 10-17. In Genesis 18: Abraham was sitting at the door of his tent, he looked and saw three men coming toward him he ran to meet them, they told him your wife Sarah is going to have a son.

In Genesis 28:10-17 we read that Jacob went out from beer-sheba, and went toward haran. He was overtaken by the night so he took a stone for his pillow, as he slept he had a dream, he saw a ladder set up on the earth, and the top of it reaches to heaven, he saw the angels of God ascending and descending on it, the dream of Jacob was no less important than that of Abraham, both were very important revelations. God was saying to Jacob I will be with you where ever you go.

Some people argue that God could reveal his will in dreams today but because of the written word of God, and the indwelling of the holy spirit have made dreams of this kind unnecessary, but this is not altogether true, because sometimes the Lord remind us of what the scripture says, like this one.

## A DREAM OF DIVINE MESSAGE DELIVERED

$\mathcal{O}$ne night I dream that I was in a very large and beautiful building, a young lady came and told me that a man was in the lobby looking for me and he said he come from God, so I ran back to the lobby but I did not see the man, so I ask the clerk that was sitting at her desk, where is the man that was looking for me, she point to a door and said he said he come from God.

So I went and knock on the door and a tall handsome young man open the door, I told him who I was and he said come in, he gave me a seat to sit and told me that he come from God and that he brought me a message, what he told me is exactly according to the words of the apostle Paul and he was not someone to take lightly, he was serious. This dream need no interpretation the message was straight forward and direct, for the people who do not have dreams of this kind do not understand the importance of a dream. I want it to be understood that God talk to his people in dreams and visions.

PSALM 25:14 teaches that the secret of the Lord is with them that fear him: and he will show them his covenant. IF I don't tell you what going on between the Lord and myself you will not have a clue, and the same thing applies to you.

## BLESSINGS TO HIM WHO FEARS THE LORD

*He will be taught by God v12*
*He will be safe and at peace v13*
*His children will be blessed v13*
*He will know God's secrets v14*
*He will know God's covenant v14*

The Lord let us know secret things that cannot be known any other way except he reveal them, we do not know what the enemy is planning to do to us but the God in whom we believe will let us know somehow. Read the third of 21 attempts to slay David 1 SAMUEL 18:8-29 how king Saul made himself an enemy of David, how the king uses his daughter Michael to trap David and have him killed, but the Lord deliver him from the king's wrath every time.

Read about one of my dream, how the Lord let me know what the enemy was planning to do. It was in 1972. The Lord uses dreams or visions to say things to us or show us things that we cannot read in the Bible, and this is one of them.

I was living at a private home, I rented a room on the second floor, there was a young lady and a young man living on the first floor, the young lady came came up from Jamaica not long before, she was home every day not working so I gave her money to buy bus ticket so she could go and look a job. My motive was pure and the Lord know that. They both leave a few months later, Then I had a dream about two weeks after they leave, in the dream I heard the door bell rang so I went down to see who it was, the young lady came back to say hi. When the young lady came in I heard the voice of the Lord said its a trick. We both went upstairs and sit down in the kitchen having a cup of coffee at that time it was about fifteen minutes, then I heard the door bell rang again it was the young man who she claim to be her brother in-law.

I wake from the dream and that same weekend they came, and it happen exactly as explain. I just sat there looking at them, until this day they don't know that the Lord let me know about their little secret plan. The Apostle Paul said if the Lord is for us who can be against us ROMANS 8:31. 1 would strongly encourage every Christian not to ignore dreams, pray and ask the Lord to help you to understand your dreams, because they are very, very important. I later found out what the trick was all about but I try to be discreet.

## WHAT ARE DREAMS

*D*reams are Revelations, the Lord uses dreams and visions to communicate with his people. He uses them in days of the patriarchs, the prophets, and in the days of the Apostles, and until this day the Lord is communicating with his people through dreams and visions.

## A DREAM OF COMMUNICATION

*S*ome years ago I invented a small musical instrument but it did not work out as I anticipated, then I had a dream that I went out to the porch of my house, in the dream I saw some tambourine in a box, so I pick up one of the tambourine and shake it, and it sound great. I woke from the dream but I could not remember how the jingles were design, that was very important for me to remember because I have never seen any tambourine jingles that beautiful, I am very sure no one make jingles like those in this life. So I prayed and ask the Lord to help me to remember how the jingles were design. I went back to bed and fell asleep, and I heard these words, if you try it one way and it did not work try it another way.

IF this is not communication I would like all the bishops and deans to tell me what was this all about. So I invented a tambourine. this was not my idea to go into the tambourine business, this was clearly the Lord.

All that I have to say about dreams, visions, and prophecy are my own true testimony of the Lord over these 40 plus years. I am a dreamer not a few hundred but thousands of them. The Lord give us dreams for many reasons. some times about our own lives, some times about a sister or brother, some times about the church, some times about the pastor, some times about a country, some times about incoming disaster, some times about heaven, some times about hell, some dreams are just too mysterious to understand, and the list goes on and on.

✧ ✧ ✧ ✧ ✧ ✧ ✧ ✧ ✧ ✧ ✧ ✧ ✧ ✧ ✧ ✧ ✧ ✧

Because of the revelation of the Lord I have proven that some things cannot be known in any other way, only the revelation of the Lord can bring them to us because such knowledge does not exist among men, no educator, no Bible school have them to teach. We cannot teach the unknown, we can only teach that which we know according to the scripture but the revelation of the Lord can let us know secret things far beyond the human knowledge and ability, if the Lord do not reveal them they cannot be known. Again I said such knowledge does not exist among men.

## A DREAM ABOUT A SISTER OF THE CHURCH THAT TURN INTO A BIRD, WHAT COULD THIS MEAN?

One night in a dream I saw a sister of the church standing in a valley of green grass, I was looking at her until she turn into a little bird, the little bird started to feed very furiously on the grass seeds in the valley, the little bird feed until it callaps and died. I ran down into the valley and picked up the little bird to see what happen to it, I examine the bird and the stomach of the bird was slit open so all the feed that the bird was eating keep flowing back out so the bird died because it could not satisfied its hunger.

The interpretation of the dream is found in JER 2:13, For my people have committed two evils, they have forsaken me the fountain of living waters, and hewed them out cisterns, broken cisterns, that can hold no water. A cistern is a tank and if that tank is leaking, one day no water will leave in it. This sister was in a backslidden condition and she died spiritually. It is very important for Christians to know the scripture so when the Lord give us certain dreams we can go to the Bible for the understanding of that dream.

Some dreams need no interpretation because they are very straightforward. I have them so I do know.

## DREAMS ARE NOT FOOLISHNESS AS SOME PEOPLE WOULD WANT YOU TO BELIEVE

(I WILL BE VERY DISCREET) Some years ago I was at a certain church and the Lord gave me a vision about a certain condition in the church so I talk about it without calling any name and a certain young lady did not came back to church for about three weeks, but I did call her to see how she was doing. she did came back and some months later one day she ask me if I remember when she did not come to church for about 2 or 3 weeks I said yes I remember, she said what I said that day was too close for COMFORT. Now she realize her deeds was no more a secret, and she come to her senses. IF it take a dream or a vision to guide us back on the right path the Lord will use them because he is not willing that any should perish but that all should come to repentance.

### A DREAM THAT WARNS ABOUT DIVORCE

Many months after the first dream the Lord gave me another dream about her, this time I was told in the dream that she would be divorce, so I went to her and told her that If she don't take step to protect her marriage she would be separated from her husband and she would be divorced. Maybe she did not believe that her husband would divorce her but it happened a few months later she was separated from her husband and then divorced.

Some church group are teaching God's people that they are not to believe in dreams, and it is because the Lord is not talking to them. I cannot see the Lord talking to a person and call his revelation foolishness, after the word of God tell us that we will dream dreams, and see visions JOEL 2;28-29:

Listen to this, one night I had a dream about a brother who is the owner of a store in our city, I called him the following morning and I said to him, I did what you ask me to do for you, he said really, I said yes I did, he ask, and that is what? so I told him, I saw

❖ ❖ ❖ ❖ ❖ ❖ ❖ ❖ ❖ ❖ ❖ ❖ ❖ ❖ ❖ ❖ ❖ ❖

you in a dream last night and you told me that when I am praying I am to mention your name, the first thing the gentleman said, and they said we are not to believe in dreams, then he told me a small part of the problem that he was having, and that tells me the rest of the story. The gentleman know that my dream was true.

The Lord want me to pray for him so I put him on my prayer list. Dreams is not an enemy they are a great friend, I said a great friend. Dreams let us know things we cannot learn in schools. The Apostle Paul had a big problem, he had a thorn in the flesh 2 COR 12:7-9 and he besought the Lord three times that it might depart from him, but the Lord did not take it away from him, he told him my grace is sufficient for thee, for my grace is made perfect in weakness. Sometimes the Lord doesn't take away the problem but he give us more grace to carry us through.

Frequently in ancient times God spoke in dreams to even to those outside the chosen family, he spake to Abimelech of Gerar (GEN 20: v3) But God came to Abimelech in a dream by night, and said to him, behold, thou art but a dead man, for the woman which thou hast taken, for she is a man's wife.

To Laban in GEN 31;v24 And God came to Laban the Syrian in a dream by night, and said unto him, take heed that thou speak not to Jacob either good or bad. Also to the butler and baker of pharaoh GEN 40:v8-19, and to pharaoh himself GEN 41:1-36 then much later to Nebuchadnezzar DAN 2:1-45,CH4:5-33 v5 I saw in a dream which made me afraid, and the thoughts upon my bed made the visions of my head troubled me. IN those dreams, the meaning was clear enough to need no interpretation, as in those of Abimelech and Laban, or else God will use one of his servant to interpret the meaning, as in later cases, one principle of interpretation is quite clear, when the symbol is in the natural realm, the interpretation is in the human realm. When Joseph dreamed of the sun, moon and eleven stars bowing to him, his brethren immediately knew the meaning as referring to his mother father and brethren GEN 37:9-1l, when the symbol is in the human realm, as in DAN 7:v8, eyes like the eyes of a man and a mouth speaking great things the interpretation is in spiritual realm.

Dreams may lead men astray, but God's word tell us how to deal with this situation- DEUT 13:1-3 IF there arise among you a prophet or a dreamer of dreams and giveth thee a sign or a wonder. And the sign sign or wonder come to pass where he speak unto thee, saying, let us go after other God's which thou hast not known, and let us serve them-Thou shalt not hearken unto the words of that prophet, or that dreamer of dreams, for the Lord your God proveth you, to know whether you love the Lord your God with all your heart and with all your soul. see also 1 JOHN

## PROTECTION OF GOD'S LOVE

*We* are commanded to test all spirit. v1 Beloved, believe not every spirit, but try the spirits whether they they are of God, because many false prophets are gone out into the world.

### HOW TO TEST THE SPIRITS

v2 Hereby know ye the spirit of God, every spirit that confesseth that Jesus Christ is come in the flesh is of God. v3 And every spirit that confesseth not that Jesus Christ is come in the flesh is not of God, and this is the spirit of antichrist, whereof ye have heard that it should come, and even now already in the world.

### HOW TO OVER COME DEMONS

v4 Ye are of God, little children and have overcome them, because greater, is he that is in you, than he that in the world..

### MARKS OF DEMON INSPIRED FALSE TEACHERS

1 TIM 6:v3, 2 TIM 3:v2, 2 Peter 2:10-22
v5 They are of the world, therefore speak they of the world, and the world heareth them.

✧ ✧ ✧ ✧ ✧ ✧ ✧ ✧ ✧ ✧ ✧ ✧ ✧ ✧ ✧ ✧ ✧

## MARKS OF TRUE CHRISTIAN

*V*6 We are of God, he that knoweth God heareth us, he that is not of God heareth not us, Hereby know we the spirit of truth, and the spirit of error.

God speaks to people today in dreams just as he did in the days of old. You may ask, really? Listen to this. I started a new church in 1981, the clerk that we started with resign the office after some months, so another clerk was appointed, who was a sister of the church. We never have any financial problem, there was always enough money in the account to cover the bills, until one night I heard the voice of the Lord in a dream said to me, check the money, when I woke from the dream I could not understand what money the Lord was talking about because there was no money problem.

About two weeks after the dream the bank manager called me and said pastor Grey, you don't have enough money in the account to cover the cheques, so I ask him, are you sure sir, he said yes I am sure.

I called the clerk and ask her did you put the money in the bank? she said yes I did, I told her I want to see the book, so we met and she go through every thing to show me what she did, the book was fine but the money was missing. She insisted she did not know what happen to the money. I told her I have to call the bishop, she said go ahead, so I call the bishop, and we had a second meeting and she still denigh knowing anything about the money. At the end of the second meeting I said to her, you take over the account with this amount of money, where is that money? the bishop said yes sister where is it? she could not lie any more, so she said she barrow the money. she paid it back. It is clear that the Lord know the money was missing and he inform me about it. To God be the glory. When Christians are on good terms with God it is amazing what he will reveals, so stay close to him in your relationship and he will stay close to you.

God is a real person and he talk to his children about real

things. Just in case you do not believe that God talk to people to-day in dreams you need to start believing.

*Do you believe God talk to sinners?*
*If you don't you are going to be very surprise*

While I was in my sinful state one night I had a dream hearing the voice of a man which was the Lord said to me get up and say your prayer, the prayer he mean was the Lord's prayer in matt 6: 9-13, that night when I woke from the dream, I was on my knees on the bed saying the prayer, I did not know when I get up, I did know when I started the prayer, all I know I found myself doing what he said. I am very sure the devil would never want me to call upon my heavenly father, IF THIS WAS NOT the Lord then who was it. I accepted the Lord about nine months after this dream.

## YOU STILL DON'T BELIEVE THAT GOD TALK TO SINNERS? LISTEN TO THIS

The Lord watches our witnessing. After I become a Christian I was talking to one of my niece about giving her heart to the Lord Jesus Christ, she was a about 13 years old at the time. She woke one morning and said to me, uncle I had a dream last night, I saw a man and he said what you are telling me is true. The Lord talk to the young lady confirming my words that they are true. It would take a fool to say that this was not God.

*Dreams are very important. Matt 2.v13,*
*v19-23 dreams are not to be ignored.*
*They carry very important messages like this one*

I had a friend who worship at another church, I saw him in a dream one night standing at a certain place, I was looking at him, and I heard the voice of the LORD said to me, tell him to continue serving me. I called him the next morning and gave him the message. May be the brother was getting discourage because he was having a lot of problems at the time.

I believe the Lord send him this message to comfort his heart to let him know he have seen his problems and that he will be with him. One would have to be out of their mind to believe that this was not God.

## IF YOU BELIEVE DREAMS ARE FOOLISHNESS I WILL ARGUE WITH YOU UNTIL THE SUN STOP SHINING

Some dreams are quite challenging to understand but the nice thing is that some of them come with a clue and if you can only remember that one clue you could understand your dream. A clue could be something you heard, see, or smell, like this one. I had a dream one night seeing a tall lady dress in full white, her dress was down to the floor, she said to me, he want you to look for it, and find it, and find it, and when you find it you will know that you find it. This dream comes with a clue, it was something I smell and I understood the dream. I could not understood the dream without that clue.

## THE LORD GUIDE US AND DELIVER US FROM SECRET DANGERS

When Christians are planning to get marry we must seek the guidance of the Lord, because you could be heading for lions den with your eyes wide open but cannot see the lions. people are not always who you are looking at they can be very different. Some times people are blinded by love and money and cannot see the danger, but the Lord will guide you if you will let him do so. The Lord is the one who know's people we don't. I heard people speak of other people how nice and wonderful and beautiful they were until they get the shock of their lives. Some people marry not for love but with a selfish desire and end up with what they did not want, misery, heartaches,they regret the day they said I do. Ladies and gentlemen it is better to be happy with little than to be miserable with plenty.

Let the word of God be your guide. The word of God teaches that godliness with contentment is great gain for we brought nothing into this world, and it is certain we can carry nothing Out. And having food and raiment let us therewith content. But they that will be rich fall into temptation and a snare, and into many foolish and hurtful lust, which drown men into destruction and perdition. For the love of money is the root of all evil which while some coveted after, they have erred from the faith, and pierced themselves through with many sorrows, l TIM 6:6-10).

## MY TRUE LOVE STORY HOW THE LORD SEND HIS ANGEL TO COME AND TALK TO ME, TO GOD BE THE GLORY

*I* am telling you all these things so you may know how important it is to let the Lord guide you. It was in 1972, I was in love with a sister of the church, she was a very humble nice lady, you could not tell me any thing about her for me to change my mind, I was in love.

Then the Lord started to give me dreams about her, dreams and more dreams, at one point I ask her about one of the dreams, she told me she will not discuss her private life, so I drop the matter because I did not want to lose her. IN another dream I saw two dogs grab her and throw her to the ground drink out all her blood until she was blue, but nothing could change my mind. Those two dogs represent unbelievers, but nothing move me.

The Lord was showing me all these things to get my attention and for me to change my mind but nothing work, I could not see the danger, but the Lord know I was heading for the lions den, but he would not stand by and see me get destroyed. So the Lord send his angel to come and talk to me, and when he was finish talking to me and said in plain english language, do not marry her, and he raise his hand to heaven and walk away.

This was a serious vision and could not be ignored. Raising his hand to heaven mean, heaven bear witness that I was told.

When I woke from the dream it was the first time I was nervous and afraid because I know the Lord had spoken. For me to tell her I could not see her any more was a very hard thing to do because she did me no harm. But to obey the Lord and be on the safe side I have no choice. I did not know how she would react, I thought she would call me creep, and bastard, but she did not. When I told her the dream she said if the Lord told you, you have to obey, she was very nice, but something was very wrong.

The lord know what is coming our way, he know what we are dealing with, so give him a chance to guide you. God know the mindset and intentions of people we don't. The Lord could give you a dream about the people you are dealing with, in order to guide you, so do not ignore a dream because your life could depend on that dream, so pay much attention to what the Lord reveals. IF you do not obey that dream you will pay the price, it happen to me so I am telling you true story and not something I read in books.

## HOW WILL THE LORD GUIDE US IN DREAMS

Listen to this. Some years ago I had an appointment with a man to come to my place so we could talk about a business plan, what I did not know is that he was coming to get money from me but the Lord know the intention of the man, so the Lord gave me a dream about the man. I saw a man came to me in the dream and ask me for some money but I did not give it to him, that was my guide. two days later the man came for the meeting, at the end of the meeting he ask me for $500 and I gave it to him and he disappear I did not get my money back, and that was many years ago.

If I did just did what the dream said by not giving him any money I would not lose my money. You believe in a God you cannot see, that's fine, that is faith, but when this same God try to guide you through a dream you cannot believe, why not? what's wrong?.

## GOD'S WORD ARE NOT FOOLISHNESS OR ELSE THEY COULD NOT BE THE WORD OF GOD

And it shall come to pass afterward, that I will pour out my spirit upon all flesh, and your sons and your daughters shall prophesy, your old men shall dream dreams, your young men shall see visions. And also upon the servants and upon the handmaids in those days will I pour out my spirit. JOEL2:28-29. ON the day of Pentecost Peter stand up and said this is it which was spoken by the prophet Joel, ACTS 2:16-17.

When the Lord did not need the ministry of the old testament priesthood any more he bring it to an end. Now Jesus is the High priest Heb 4:14-15, Seeing then that we have a great high priest that is passed into the heavens, Jesus the son of God, let us hold fast our profession. For we have not an high priest which cannot be touched with the feeling of our infirmities, but was in all points tempted like we are yet without sin.

## AND WE ARE THE ROYAL PRIESTHOOD I PETER 2:V9

But ye are a chosen generation a royal priesthood, an holy nation a peculiar people, that ye should show forth the praises of him who hath called you out of darkness into his marvellous light.

When the lord did not need the ministry of the prophets any more he bring it to an end, The ministry of the prophets are no longer with us, but the gift of prophecy is still with us in the church. Prophecy is one of the gift of the spirit I COR 12:v10. The Lord did not bring dreams and visions to an end, it is alive and well in the church.

## DREAMS FOREWARN US OF HIDDEN DANGERS

I know a sister of the church who finish Bible school and was to take up her first pastoral minis try, the Lord gave me a dream about her, in the dream I was told that the devil was waiting for her where she was going. I went to her and told her that the devil was waiting for her there. She leave the following week, and about six or seven months later she came back home, it happen to her. The Lord will inform us of the plans of the devil, but it is up to us not fall into his trap, the devil will always setting traps to catch the righteous, but the Lord expect us to use our god given brain and be wise, especially when we are warned. A Christian would be very foolish not to take dreams seriously. The Lord will not always talk to us personally, sometimes he will send one of his servant to come and talk to you, so please, please pay attention.

## A LADY WHO IGNORE HER DREAMS

$\mathcal{I}$ know of a lady who told me two of her dreams. This lady was living at an apartment building at the time, she said she had a dream one night hearing the foot steps of a soldier coming up the stairs and came and knock on her door. When she open her door there was this man dress like a soldier, he said to her I was trying to get to you a long time but I could not.

The question is, what happen now why he was able to get to her? answer) she invite him there. That soldier is the devil. The dream have to do with her deeds.

Dream#2. She told me that she had a dream one night seeing a man hand her a bill of divorce. When she told me that I know the woman was going to be divorce. These two dreams link to each other, they were dreams of warning to let her know if she continue the course that she was on she would be divorce. She ignore her dreams and she was divorce years later just as the dream reveals to her, she receive that bill of divorce.

## GOD STILL ASK HIS PEOPLE QUESTION IN DREAMS

$\mathcal{A}$fter I was filled with the Holy Ghost in my home church, I started to preach because I called to preach. One night in a dream I heard the voice of the Lord ask me this question, do you think you can manage a church?I told him I don't know sir, you would have to try me first. I told my pastor the dream I had, he smile and said l have already spoken to a district pastor that I know to find a church to put you. About 5 or 6 weeks later I was sent to pastor my first church. IF you do not believe that God talk to Christians today you and I are not on the same page.

## GOD WANT TO DEAL WITH PEOPLE WHO WILL BELIEVE HIM

$\mathcal{O}$ne of the worst sin Israel committed was the sin of unbelief And the Lord was very angry with them for this sin. christians must believe all of God's word whether we understand them or not, we do not have luxury to believe what we want and throw the rest in the trash basket.

## GOD KNOW HOW WE LIVE

$\mathcal{A}$bout 8 weeks after I was at my new church, one night the Lord spoke to me in a dream and said, these people are an out of order people and the lives they live are rogug-rug which mean very bad, There were three deacons in the church and the Lord told me in a dream that one of them is like the sons of ELI, ELI was a high priest, who had two sons, Hophni and phinehehas, 1 SAMUEL 3:v 13, ELI knew that his sons was not living for the Lord and he let them run wiled, he did not restrained them, they were vile.

I did not know which one the Lord was talking about but I later found out which one he was talking about and it was true. THE Lord will always be right.

## WELCOME TO SECRETS OF CHRISTIAN DREAMS

$\mathcal{T}$he Lord will let us know secret and evil plans of others-again there were three deacons in the church that I pastor, and one night the Lord gave me a dream of all three deacons. I saw them sit down and engaged-in a conversation over me, the conversation was a plot against me, the Lord let me hear every word they said. When I woke from the dream I think about it and I want to tell the church about the dream but I could not tell the church about the dream, then you may ask, why not? here is the reason, the Lord constrain me so that I could not talk about it, and it was for a very good reason. About 2 or 3 weeks after this dream I felt free to tell the clerk of the church. When I told her she looked as if she was standing on another planet, she was shocked to know that I know the conversation and I was not there. The lady said to me, I know none of those men told you, how did you know this?

I told her the Lord reveal it to me in a dream. She said to me as long as you are here never to said a word about this dream because if those men know that you know about this conversation my husband are going to be in big trouble with those men that is him tell you. What her husband have to do with it (nothing) her husband was there in the meeting and he was the only one that was not in agreement with them, so any how they know that I know about the conversation I could not convince them that it was the Lord that reveal it to me and that innocent man would be in serious trouble with them. The Lord did not show me the forth man because he was not a part of the plot. So I stayed at that church until I leave and I never said a word about that dream.

Ladies and gentlemen, the Lord watches the Lord pays attention, much attention so whatever you do let it be honest and fair and not according to our own agenda because the Lord shall bring every work into judgment whether they are good or evil. ECCL 12:vi4. I don't think some people realize how much the Lord will reveal in order to protect his people and make us wise so we can escape the trap of the enemy, the Lord uses dreams and visions to put us on our guard.

A SONG

$\mathscr{I}$need thee every hour, most gracious Lord, no tender voice like thine can peace afford. I need thee o 1 need thee, every hour I need thee, o bless me now, my saviour, I come to thee,

Never be too hasty to talk about certain dreams, some dreams are very sensitive and need wisdom to deal with them. A person who do not know how to control their tongue can do more harm than good, wisdom is needed.

## A DREAM THAT CALLS FOR WISDOM

$\mathscr{L}$isten to this and you will see what I mean. what I mean. Some years ago the Lord gave me a dream about a member of the church, he took me into their house and showed me what was going on, There were two girls living there among other children. I send a message to one of the girls, the one that belong to the husband to be very careful careful because something is about to happen. About thirty days later the mother call me and ask me to come to the home to pray with them and that she have something she want to talk to me about. I went to the home and what she told me I could not tell her the dream I had thirty days before, if I did, it would confirm what she believe all a long and that would be the end of the marriage. wisdom is needed.

Dreams are very important in the life of a believer, the Lord uses them to inform us or forewarn us, they are too important to be taken lightly.

A SONG

$\mathscr{C}$arry on for Jesus every where you go, let the hope of glory be the seed you sow, like a streaming beacon thru the darkest night, guiding souls a right, carry on for Jesus as you go, carry on for him while here below, step by step when rugged path are dim, carry on for him.

## THE LORD SHOWED ME THE WORK OF A WITCHCRAFT WORKER

*I*ts not every body can believe that you can dream about something and wake up in the morning and go look for it and expect to find it. AS a dreamer I learn to believe God, I have seen too many results for me to doubt. About six months after I was at my first church, one night the Lord took me into the church in a dream and showed me two coins on the floor of the rostrum and one coin in one of the kneeling pad. I got up the morning and went up to the church and look for the money and found it but it was not on the rostrum floor, it was covered up on the pulpit stand. The pulpit stand was covered with a very soft nice plastic and that's where they put the money. There were no money in the kneeling pad, the coin that I saw in the kneeling pad was only a clue, meaning that the money was covered up, and so it was.

IF a person can figure out what certain clues mean, you could understand many dreams. Dreams are true so believe God as he give his revelations.

## HEAD KNOWLEDGE IS GOOD BUT IT IS NOT ENOUGH WE NEED TO HEAR FROM GOD

*I*N these days too many religious leaders depend on their head knowledge, but head Knowledge cannot let us know all the secret plans of the devil, but the revelation of the Lord can, the revelation of the Lord will let us know what we cannot learn in Bible school or any other school because on one have such knowledge to teach, it does not exist. what we need is the anointing power of the Holy spirit on our lives.

A SONG

*W*hen we walk with the Lord in the light of word, what a glory he sheds on our way, while we do his good will, he abide with us still, and with all who will trust and obey. Trust and obey, for there is no other way to be happy in Jesus, but to trust and obey.

## AFTER A VICTORY DO NOT RELAX THE DEVIL AND HIS DEMONS WILL BE PLANNING FOR YOU

For you who do not believe that the devil is a real demon I want you to read this article very carefully. IN 1968 1 was in the Bahamas Island for about nine months, at the house where I was staying a lady was violently sick one sunday evening. She believe she was poison, she was in the kitchen looking about some food to have supper and a sudden pain hit her in the chest area, so she leave everything on the kitchen table and went to her room. About two minutes after that a brother went to her room to see how she was doing, he rush back to me and said the lady was dying, so I took my Bible and went to her room and read from JAMES 5:14-15 about praying for the sick, at this point she was not around she was drifting out of herself, I took her by the hand and pray for her healing, and she came back immediately and said its gone its gone, I ask her what is gone? she said I was going to die, I was going to die, I was cold and I was drifting away so I know I was going to die.

She said she was going to the doctor just to see what did happen to her, so I ask her if she believe that the Lord healed her, she said yes, so I told her the doctor will not find anything so she was to keep her money, so she did not go to see the doctor.

## A SECOND HEALING

When I went home from church that sunday night another lady that was living in the same house called me to pray for one of her hand, she saw what happen a few hours before and her faith grows, she said she could not use her hand for months. I ask her what happen to her hand she said she believe she catch cold in it. I pray for her healing that night two days later I ask her how is your hand now? she said its ok now.

The monday morning a man was healed of a very bad pain in his back.

## THE DEVIL SHOWED UP AFTER THE HEALING

One week after the healing the devil approach me in a dream in the form of a very large black man, very black, he said to me, I heard you heal three people, I ask him who tell you that? he gave me a very funny name of which I believe was one of his demons-In the dream I began to talk to him about Jesus but he did not want to hear that, so he walk away and said, it might soon leave you, he mean the healing power, I said to him it don't have to leave. At that time I Was about 4 1/2 years old as a Christian.

## THE ASSAULT BEGINS, THE DEVIL MEAN BUSINESS

The devil cannot be taken lightly, he is a vicious and dangerous enemy. If you do not mean business with God you will be just a puppet in his hands. I know the devil was around but I have never experience such vicious attack until after the healing. The devil know I was a danger to his cause so he want to get rid of me, the things that were no problem before has now become a big problem but thank God I overcome. Peter said, Casting all your care upon him, for he careth for you. be sober, be vigilant, or watchful, because your adversary the devil, as a roaring lion, walking about, seeking whom he may devour. Whom resist steadfast in the faith, knowing that the same afflictions are accomplished in your brethren that are in the world, I Peter 5:7-9).

## THE ASSAULT CONTINUES

It is very important that a Christian life are very dedicated unto the Lord so that he can talk to us and guide us in our struggle, at one point in the fight the Lord spoke to me, I was under attack and the Lord spoke to me and let me know what was happening, I heard these words in a night vision, the devil is doing everything to destroy you, when I heard words like those it causes me to dig my heels in and fight to win, to fight the good fight of faith and to lay hold on eternal life. It is like a boxer in a boxing ring defending his championship belt against the challenger, after a few rounds he went back to his corner, the champion need to know if he is winning the fight, so they told him you are two points behind in the fight. A few words of wisdom and encouragement from his corner is very important, now he know what he have to do, they told him stay off the ropes and do not back up, you must take the fight to the guy or else you will be going home without the belt-For a person who say they are a Christian and do not believe that the Lord talk to his people through a dream or a vision is beyond my understanding.

To take away a champion belt is more than words, you will have to fight him and beat him, its not a cake walk, one will have to be tough and better than the champion. We are the champion, the devil have no more power over us than what we give him. Greater is he that is in us than he that is in the world 1 JOHN 4:v4.

A SONG

*I*'ve seen the lightening flashing, and heard thunder roll, I've felt sins brakers dashing trying to conquer my soul. I've heard the voice of my saviour, telling me still to fight on He promised never to leave me, never to leave me alone.

NO never alone, no never alone He promised never to leave me never to leave me alone, no never alone,no never alone He promised never to leave me, never to leave me alone.

## TO BELIEVE THAT GOD TALK TO PEOPLE TODAY IS VERY NICE, BUT TO KNOW IS EVEN BETTER

*You* may ask what I mean, this is what I mean. To believe means to regard as true or real, or have faith in.

To know means, to be aware of something, to have information about someone, to be acquainted with someone, or recognize someone or or something, to have experience, or you understanding. IN my case I know God talk to people today because he talk to me. Sometimes when a fight is over the champion have swollen eyes and bloody-nose, but he won, and that is the most important part of the fight, therefore fight to win. The Christian life is not a simple one, there are challenges, road blocks, set backs, but in all these things the Apostle Paul said we are more than conquerors through him that love us ROMANS 8:v37.

## THE DEVIL TALK TO CHRISTIANS IN DREAMS TOO

$\mathcal{S}$ome years ago I had a dream that I was walking on a road and there was a big black man walking on another road that run parallel to my road Both roads were divided with a wire fence and a small strip of land. I notice the man was watching me, so he step over the wire fence and rush over on my road and said to me, do you know when you are depending on someone to do things for you and they wont do it, do you know how that feels? I said no I don't. And he became very angry and pull his sword on me and swipe at me, he was viciously serious and wanted to kill me, I slip the sword and grab it and hang on to it, so we struggle and struggle) he was strong but I was just as strong. When he could not get the sword away from me his sword turned into a serpent, I was hanging on to the middle area of the serpent and he was hanging on to the neck area of the serpent, and pushing the serpent head down to my hand saying sting him, sting him, at that point somebody throw me a sword, I grab it with my right hand and swipe at the serpent head, and I wake from the dream.

If you have not fought with this serpent you will not know what it mean to fight with the devil and live. The sword in my right hand is the word of God. The Lord was letting me know that when I fight him with the word he cannot win. DAVID said, Thy word have I hid in mine heart, that I might not sin against thee.

## THE DEVIL GET NOTHING DONE WITHOUT OUR HELP, SO WHY HELP HIM?

*T*he devil know he did not have me any more he know he could not depend on me so he was mad and wanted to kill me: And every one that name the name of christ must be watchful because he will fight you just the same. The Lord knows what is coming so he will give us a dream to inform us or forewarn us so we can be watchful. The devil is not our friend, he is an enemy, I hated him because he have my friends and love ones trap in sin to take them to hell with him, so how can he be a friend? you may say he is not your friend either but if you are doing the things that he want you to do he see you as friends, all the devil need is to get people to help him do his dirty work.

The Apostle Paul said, know ye not that to whom ye yield yourselves servants to obey, his servants ye are to whom ye obey, whether of sin unto death, or obedience unto righteousness ROMANS 6:v16

## HOW BEAUTIFUL IT WOULD BE IF THE DEVIL DID NOT HAVE ANY FRIENDS IN THE CHURCH

*I*t would be a wonderful feeling to know that all the people who said they are Christian were true Christians, but it is sad to say that not every one are true Christian some are secret sinners in the church, the life they live are an invitation to the devil because you are a servant to whom you obey, they are employees of the devil doing the work of their master the devil. And who are these people, you may ask, they are those who slander their brother and sister in the Lord, they are talebearers, people who carry news against one another, they are traitors, they are disloyal, they will give you away for less than thirty pieces of silver, they are fornicators, adulterers, and all manner of evil works-AS long as the devil can get you to help him do his dirty work he will be very happy and call you friends.

I discover that when the Lord want us to know certain things he let us know them., Not long ago I was worshipping at a certain church and one night I had a dream, in the dream I was talking with a man about the church and the people I was worshipping with, I was telling him how loving, and sincere, and dedicated the people were, and he said some of them, if the Lord did not see the rest of them as being loving, sincere, and dedicated, then they are in trouble and need to examine themselves to see whether they are in the faith or not. Paul said, Wherefore we labour, that, whether present or absent, we may be accepted of him. 2 Cor 5:9)

## AND WHEN THE SPIRIT OF TRUTH IS COME

The Lord have many things to say to us and to show us, some of these things you cannot read them in the Bible in details because they have to do with our every day lives, such as our workplace, the people we are dealing with, places we are going, sometimes a message for someone, and the list goes on and on, he is our comfort and guide. Any one tells you that the Lord only talk to us from the written word do not believe them it is not true because the Lord also talk to us through dreams and visions. It is not in the devils interest for any one to believe God, so he fill the hearts of many with fear, unbelief, and doubts.

NO one knows how the Lord will respond in order to protect and deliver his children, the people who do not have these revelations do not know how real these things can be. JOEL the prophet said that we are going to dream dreams and see visions, and that we will prophesy JOEL 2:28-29. There is not one Bible scholar on the planet that can tell us what we are going to dream or the visions we are going to see, or what we are going to prophesy about, because preaching is not the only way we prophesy.

And yet some people criticize these God given revelations as if they know what God would reveal, how can a person criticize something they do not understand criticism is satanic, the devil use criticism to humiliate and shut up God's people so that they don't say the things that the Lord want them to say. The devil do not want people to believe the revelation of the Lord, Jesus said when the spirit of truth is come he will show us things to come. Those who practice criticism are being used of the devil. Some people believe that to prophesy is to preach the gospel but this is only a part of it because there are people in the church today who prophesy just like the prophets, we speak of the future and those things come to pass I am one of them, I will tell you more later.

## THE LORD CAN GIVE US WORDS OF COMFORT THAT NO ONE ELSE CAN GIVE

If you don't believe this one I give up on you,(smile) for those who do not believe that God really talk to people today in dreams will finally believe this one.

Listen to these marvellous words. one night in a dream I heard these words, the Lord said to tell you your sins are forgiven. The Lord want me to know that there was nothing on my record and he let me know that, the Lord did not want me to have any doubt where I stand with him. you may ask, would the Lord talk to a person and let them know their sins were forgiven? I will ask you a question, do you believe the devil would send me this message? IF you can answer the question honestly you have answered your question. IF the Lord love this world with such perfect love that he send his only son to die in our place, why would any one want to believe that God would not talk to his own son or daughter in this manner in order to comfort them and restore confident?. IF you do not believe this dream I forgive you and will pray for you.(smile)

A SONG

I hear thy welcome voice, that calls me Lord to thee, for cleansing in thy precious blood that flowed on calvary, I am coming

Lord! coming now to thee! wash me cleanse me in the blood that flowed on calvary!

## WELCOME TO THE SCHOOL OF DREAMS

$\mathcal{D}$O not believe it will not happen to you because you think it is just a dream, that is when you will be very wrong. I was working for a company in 1979, and I had a dream seeing myself loosing one finger, so I try to be very careful on the job because I know how real my dreams can be. AS a Christian I know the Lord watches over us and will let us know about what we cannot see, hear, or know about, many dreams are forerunners, they in form us or forewarn us, so about 4 or 5 weeks after the dream I had an accident loosing one finger, just as I saw in the dream.

The devil waited until I forget, and then use a worker to trip the machine on my hand, but he did not get away, a few years later he lost a foot, the Lord avenge him.

The Lord protect my job by sending me back to work. Any one who called themselves a Christian and do not believe that God talk to people today in dreams have lost their mind.

After the accident I was off the job for about nine months, then one night in a dream I heard the voice of the Lord said to me its time to go back to work, I woke the morning and call my employer and told them that I was coming back to work monday morning. When I WENT BACK TO WORK THAT MONDAY MORNING THE union representative said to me you are very lucky bob, I ask why? he said the company was planning to let you go because they said you may not be able to manage the job any more. The Lord know what they were planning to do so he send me back to work, because he did not want me to loose my job. IF you do not believe that the Lord talk to people today in dreams I will ask the Lord to help your unbelief.

## THE LORD REVEAL THE FUTURE OF THE COMPANY TO ME IN A DREAM

*I* continue to work for the company, then one night I dream that I went to work on the after noon shift, and I did not see the plant, just the plain ground where the plant was. Then I saw a man passing by, so I ask him what happen to the plant and he said they move it away. when I woke from the dream I know the plant was going to be closed. When I went to work that day I told the workers that the company was going to be closed. They laugh me to scorn. They ask me if I was ok, they believe I was loosing my mind. About 2 1/2 years later we get the letter that the plant would be closed in six months, then the workers said to me you were right Bob you were right. There was another preacher that was working there and heard my prediction. A few months after the plant was closed he passed by, he called me and said, you will have to go and see your vision. SO I went to see for myself and it was exactly as the Lord showed it me, the plant was gone leaving the plain ground. The man in the dream told me they move it away and that is exactly what happen, they move the operation of the company to another city about sixty miles away.

There are people who are ready to find all kinds of fault and criticize dreams, but if the Lord said so that is the way it will be. ISAIAH the prophet said, For as the rain cometh down, and snow from heaven, and returneth not thither, but watereth the earth, and maketh it bring forth bud, that it may give seed to the sower, and bread to the eater. SO shall my word be that goeth forth out of my mouth. It shall not return unto me void, but it shall accomplish to that which I please, and it shall prosper in the things whereto I sent it ISAIAH 55:10-11)

❖ ❖ ❖ ❖ ❖ ❖ ❖ ❖ ❖ ❖ ❖ ❖ ❖ ❖ ❖ ❖

## THE LORD SHOWED ME MYSELF AS AN EAGLE WHAT COULD THIS MEAN?

$\mathcal{M}$any years ago when I came to Canada, one night the lord gave me a dream of a man who gave me tour through a bird sanctuary. When we reach to a certain cage that hold a very large eagle, he stop and point to the bird and said you are that eagle. As you know a cage is no place for an eagle. These birds are born to fly high into the heavens. At that time I was not doing anything for the Lord where my ministry was concern. SO the Lord gave me this dream to let me know that the situation that I was in was no place for me to be as a preacher.

## WHEN THE SITUATION CHANGE I SAW THE EAGLE AGAIN

$\mathcal{A}$ few years later the situation changed, I was pastoring a new church that I started in 1981, and the Lord gave me a dream of the eagle again. This time the eagle was coming from heaven. I HEARD the sound of a jet plane, and I keep looking but the plane was very high, I could not see the plane for quite a while but I KEEP looking until it was now in sight, but it was not a plane it was the eagle coming from heaven. The flight of an eagle is silent, so the Lord uses the sound of the plane to alert me because he want me to hear it coming. The eagle came down and landed on the ground about 25 feet from me, I picked up the bird and shout O my eagle my eagle. Now the eagle was free to live out its full potential because it was now free and no more sitting in a cage, so likewise I was now free because I was pastoring a church doing what the Lord called me to do.

The Lord uses illustrations to convey his message so if you are not alert and sensitive towards dreams you will miss the message. SO people would criticize these beautiful dreams because they do not understand the message that they brings. IF you do not understand your dreams tell somebody who can help you with the understanding.

# THE LORD PUT ME ON FASTING AND PRAYER

*S*ometimes what we called a dream are not dreams, some are visions because visions have to do with seeing, so when you dream about real things that need no interpretation or very little interpretation you could have a vision and not a dream. When you read this article You will see what I mean because dreams are illustrations.

I will be very discreet here to avoid revealing certain party, it was a time when I was dealing with certain people and the person was working against me but I did not know until the Lord started to talk to me concerning the person. One sunday I went home from church, I was sitting on the sofa, and I fell asleep for about 3 or 4 minutes and I heard the voice of the Lord called the person name to me and said his mind is not good. I went to church and I looked at him but I did not say any thing to the person because the Lord only want me to know the inner part of the person. We do not know what people are thinking but the Lord who knows our hearts he can reveal these things to us so that we can be wise when dealing with them. I thought I was dealing with a friend and a brother in the Lord but the Lord let me know how wrong I was.

It was not long after this vision the Lord gave me a second vision about the same person again. IN the dream the Lord told me that the person change his mind. what was this all about? we had an agreement and when he break it the Lord let me know about it. Jesus said, again I say unto you, that if two of you shall agree on earth as touching any thing that they shall ask, it shall be done for them of my father which is in heaven matt 18:19).1 went to church and I said to him, so you change your mind, and he ask, about what? so I said to him we had an agreement but you change your mind, his reply was, I don't know what the Lord want me to do yet. He did not deny what I said because he know he did change his mind just as the lord said. And it was after this vision I heard the voice of Lord in a dream said to me you have to fast, so I put myself on fasting for a while. I did not know why the Lord put me on fasting.

Just after I break the fast the Lord spoke to me again in a night vision and said you have to pray, its not that I was not praying but he want me to keep praying because he know trouble was coming and he want me to stay strong in order to go through the storm. I did not fully understand all this until when things went wrong. It was then then I understood why the Lord put me on fasting and prayer. When this was all over the Lord showed him to me again in a night vision on his knees praying, the Lord let me heard the words of his prayer, he was asking the Lord to forgive him for what he did to me. The Lord want me to know he was the one that did it. When two of us agree to do any thing for the Lord Jesus Christ we must keep craftiness out of it because the Lord has become an equal partner in that agreement. Ladies and gentlemen these are vision and not dreams because they need no interpretation. Visions also come while you are wide awake.

(Because) except the Lord build the house, they labour in vain that build it. Except the Lord keep the city, the watchman waketh but in vain PSALM 127:vi) Blessed is every one that feareth the Lord, that walketh in his ways PSALM 128: Vi) The Lord will stand by those that walketh uprightly.

## THE LORD REMIND ME ABOUT A TAMBOURINE

It was about two years before I invented a tambourine one night in a dream I found myself on a very large beautiful green lawn, the property had a very large beautiful house on it and some men was working on the third floor. and I heard the voice of the LORD call me, he said, Robert, I answer and said yes Sir I am here, and he said its Jesus, I was very exited, I was jumping up and I was saying o my Lord where are you, I was trying to see him because he was up there with the men but I not see him, and he said invention and I know he was talking about the tambourine, so I invented a tambourine.

## THE LORD CLEAR THE WAY FOR ME

*A*fter I invented the tambourine, one night I found myself travelling on a very lonely road, there was no houses any where in sight there was no one any where, but I travel until at last there was one house by the side of road. I knock on the door of the house but no one answer, the door was bolted shut and a fence around the house so no one could get in, it was well secured. But my faith was very strong and I looked at the bolted door and said in the name of Jesus open up, and the nuts on bolts fell off on the floor inside the house so I just use my fingers and pull the bolts out and open the door.

When the door was open I saw 4 or 5 men in the back talking I CALL to them, and when the owner of the house saw me he was mad, he was furious and said to one of the men did I not told you to lock that door, and he said I did but the owner of the house pull his gun and shoot the man. The owner was satan the men are evil spirits that work for him. After he shoot the man he came out on the road to talk to me with the rest of men, he was still arguing with the men and was going to shoot another one so I stop him at that point. I said to him don't shoot the man, the door was locked but Jesus showed me how to open it, and I said to him in the name of Jesus get down on your belly and he was down on all four and I tied his hands behind his back.

And after I did that, just a mind said look over your head and when I did there was Jesus over us in the air about 40 feet up looking down on us. I was filled with great joy when I saw him. And he did what he did on the mount of transfiguration, he was transfigured before my eyes his robe was as white as snow, but his face did not shine. Dreams are a marvellous source of inspiration and encouragement to a child of God. When I wake from the dream I catch myself singing this song.

## MY SAVIOUR'S LOVE

*I* stand amazed in the present of Jesus the nazarene and wonder how he could love me a sinner condemned, unclean.

(chorus) How marvelous! how wonderful! and my song shall ever be: how marvelous how wonderful is my saviour's love for me!

It is amazing to me to see how God can give us these marvelous dreams and yet there are people who say they are Christians and having problems believing that dreams and visions are one of God ways that he use to communicate with his children. I would like to know what kind of dreams these people are having if any, why they don't want god's people to believe in dreams. This must be a plan of the devil to stop God's people from believing that God is dealing with them in dreams. It must be noted that the dreams of the sinner is not the same as the dreams of the righteous because God is dealing with the righteous in ways that he is not dealing with the sinner. All dreams does not mean the same thing for ever one.

## BEFORE THE WORLD TRADE CENTER IN THE U.S.A. WAS HIT

*I* had a dream about thirty days before the world trade center in the united states of America was hit. I dream that I was on a half finish high rise building. I was standing on a balcony many floors up, and I saw a potion of earth blow up quite violently and it was travelling at a very high speed, the blow up was not like the way we know it, it continue going at a very high speed, and the apartment building keep turning around with me so I could watch, the smoke was very black and very high it filled the skys. I looked at the blowing up of the earth in amazement, until I saw a rope came down from heaven about 100 feet from the building that I was on.

I came down from off the building and ran to the rope, the rope was attach to the heavens, so I held on to the rope and tug on it just a little, and a very large piece of the heaven ripped out and fell to the ground away from where I was standing.

I went to see the pieces of the heavens that fell to the earth and it was black and looking more like pieces of asphalt and it burn up the ground where it fell.

## A MAP OF A COUNTRY

$\mathcal{T}$he area where the piece of the heaven ripped out from a map of a city or country was now there. It was marked out by very tiny lights, very beautiful. That was the world trade center blown up and crumbled to the ground. Remember when the symbol is in the natural realm, the interpretation is in the human realm. Many dreams are filled with symbols so to understand them you must pay attention to the symbols that are used in order to understand them.

## THIS IS THE INTERPRETATION OF THE DREAM

$\mathcal{T}$he blowing up of earth is the destruction of the buildings, the black smoke in the dream is the smoke from the buildings, the pieces of the heavens that fell to the earth are the buildings that crumbled to the ground, that beautiful map in the heavens represent the united states of America. This-is how the Lord describe the united states of America, with a beautiful map.

## WHAT DOES IT MEAN TO DREAM ABOUT WHITE FLOWERS

$\mathcal{D}$reams do reveal those things that are hidden from human senses, IN the year 2007 1 had a dream, seeing a brother in the Lord who told me that he was going to Jamaica to deliver some white flowers, so I told him the dream I had, he said he was in the process of doing so. The young man was planning to get married.

So to dream of white flowers mean's wedding or marriage.

## LET'S TALK ABOUT ANGELS

*Y*ou may ask what angels look like? From my own experience I can tell you that they look just like a man in features no different, only that they are spirit beings. one night in a dream I saw a potion of the heavens blocked with them. They are very handsome, and they all wore long flowing white robes, and they all had a bright shining silver trumpet at there mouth ready to blow. They were tens of thousands of them, it was truly a glorious sight, words cannot describe how glorious it was, it is truly beyond words.

## (A VISION) HAVE YOU EVER LOOK AT AN ANGEL IN REAL LIFE?

*W*e read in PSALM 34:v7 The angel of the Lord encampeth round about them that fear him, and delivereth them. Angels are real spirit beings around us but we are not seeing them. The Bible have much to say about angels. I would like you to sit down to read what I am about to tell you because your knees may get weak. It was in the early 1980s, I woke one morning, the bed room door was open, the mirror on the dresser in the bed room faces the bed room door, so while on the bed if I look into the mirror I could see anyone entering the bed room, or going to the washroom, they would be in plain sight. That morning when I woke I looked into the mirror and there was a man standing in front of the bed room door in the passage way, I looked at him for about thirty seconds, he was standing there with his hands folded before him looking into the bed room, he was the most handsome man I have ever seen. I did not turn around to look at him, I look at him through the mirror. By just looking at him standing there I know he was a guardian.

His skin was like the finest tan leather there is, he was about 5'11" to 6 feet tall. One of my three boys was going to the wash room, so when he saw the boy coming he move out of way for for the kid to pass and I did not see him any more. I would like God's people to understand that when you are alone tell yourself that you are not alone because the angel of the Lord are there watching over you but you cannot see them. I am not telling you these things because I think so, I know that, the Bible said so and it is true.

## HAVE YOU EVER HEARD ANGELS TALK IN REAL LIFE?

*T*his is another vision about angels. Some time between 1979 and 1980, one morning my wife came home from her midnight shift, she send the boys off to school and came to bed. I was still sleeping. When I woke that morning I heard voices in the living room, at first I thought the tv was on but it was not the tv, I raise my head off the pillow and listen. I heard terms that I never heard before. I heard these words, every sickness is sin and every sin is like an elephant, and another one answer and said, that's true, and they began to name names of diseases that would come. I heard many names, so when I heard of aids, bird flue, and others they are no mystery to me I expect them. Some people are blaming God for all the problems in the world, but God cannot be blamed, sin is the problem, and sin must be blamed, and except man repent, man will pay the price for for their sin.

So when I did not heard them any more I get up very quietly and tip toe to the living room to see them, but no one was there.

Not every one can believe these things, but this I can tell you; the Lord is my witness, and I lie not, all what I write in this book concerning my dreams, visions, and prophecy are the facts.

There are some who claim to be Christians will choose to glorify the devil with their unbelief, they will say he did not heard any thing, or he did not see any thing they cannot give God the glory by saying to God be the glory. This is exactly what the devil want, is to get God's people not to believe the revelation of the

Lord. THE thing that struck me is to here people say I don't believe it or to say it did not happen, even when they have no knowledge of the matter, it takes a demon to do that.

## A VISION OF THE HAND OF THE LORD

*I*t is just amazing what a vision can reveal, we do not know what the Lord will reveal until he reveal them. It was in the year 2007, I woke one morning and when I open my eyes I saw a large hand over me as I lie there on my bed. I lie there on my back and looked at that strong arm for about 10 or 12 seconds and it disappear through a window by the bed. After seeing the hand of the Lord it remind me of the hand that Belshazzar king of Babylon saw writing on the wall, mene, mene, tekel, upharsin, you have been weighed in the balances, and art found wanting. The difference here is that the hand of the Lord was there for my protection and not for harm DAN 5:25-28.

Jesus said he will be with us always even to the end of the world matt 28:20. The Lord showed me his hand from the shoulder down assuring me that he is with me as he had promise when all friends are gone and it look as if no one cares I can assure you that you have a friend on whom you can depend, the man Christ Jesus, the only true friend.

(VISIONS) The Bible dictionary declares that it is impossible to draw a sharp line of demarcation between dreams and visions. There are various hebrew, and Greek, words for this word, all came from the roots having to do with seeing visions in the Bible were for the most part given to individuals, and were not apprehended by others. Through them God revealed to seers truth in pictorial form. They cannot be seen by others except the person to whom the Lord reveal it to. So don't say I don't believe it, because you cannot know that.

Visions can come under various circumstances, in men's waking hours, DANIEL 10:v7 said, And I Daniel alone saw the vision-but a great quaking fell upon them, so they fled to hide themselves. Acts 9.v7 And the men which journeyed with him stood speechless, hearing a voice but seeing no man (by day) Acts 10: 1-4 There was a certain man in caes-a-rea called cor-ne-lius a centurion of the band called the Italian band a devout man, and one that feared God with all his house, which gave much alms to the people, and prayed to God always He saw a vision evidently about the ninth hour of the day an angel of God coming in to him, and saying unto him, cor-ne-lius. And when he looked on him, he was afraid, and said, what is it Lord? and he said unto him, thy prayers and thine alms are come up for a memorial before God. or by night, GEN 46:v2 And God spake unto Israel in a vision of the night, and said, Jacob,Jacob, and he said, here am I.

IN the old testament, there were non-writing prophets also and they were recipient of visions also ISAIAH 1: v1, OBADIAH 1:v1, NAHUM 1: v1, 2 SAMUEL 7:v17, 1 KINGS 22:17-19, 2 CHRON 9:v29, with perhaps one exception NUMBERS 24: v4. They were given only to holy men in the service of the Lord and those of a revelatory nature were all recognized as coming from GOD. IN the new testament LUKE especially show great interest in visions LUKE 1: v22, Acts 9:v10, said, And there was a certain disciple at damascus, named Ananias, and he said, behold, I am here Lord.

Acts 18:v9-10, Then spake the Lord to Paul in the night by a vision be not afraid, but speak, and hold not thy peace for I am with thee, and no man shall set on thee to hurt thee, for I have much people in this city. Biblical visions involved both immediate situations and more distant ones connected with the development of the kingdom of God. AS can be seen in the writings of ISAIAH, EZEKIEL, HOSEA, MICAH, DANIEL and JOHN. IN the old testament false prophets feigned visions and were condemned by JEREMIAH, JERE 14:v14, JERE 23:v16, and EZEK 13:v7. False prophets make up their visions they said the Lord said when he did not say anything.

Visions are marvellous, they let us know things we could not normally know or see. I have them so I am giving you the facts.

## A VISION OF A YOUNG GIRL STANDING IN MID AIR

Some years ago I went to a church to preach, while sitting there that sunday morning I saw a young girl about 12 years old standing in mid air over the congregation, with one foot on one side of the wall and the other foot on the other side of the wall. After the service I ask the pastor brother who she was, he said she was a very out of order young lady. SO from the position in which she was standing explain who she was, This is how the Holy spirit let me know who she was,(out of order),

## A VISION OF A MAN FALLEN FROM A TREE

I visit a church one sunday morning and as I was sitting there, I saw a man fallen from a tree, so I turn to the man that was sitting beside me and ask him if he was a Christian, he said no he was a backslider, so I told him the vision I saw, and I told him that the Lord want him to come back to him. The Lord want me to talk to him, so he show me a man fallen from a tree, meaning that the man that is sitting beside me is fallen from grace. I have visions of this kind before so I was quick to understand the vision. we do not know any thing about the people that sit beside us sunday after sunday, but the Lord who know their every day situations can give us a dream or a vision to help them in their struggles, Some people have rivers to cross mountains to climb and valleys to go through. So when the Lord give you a dream or a vision they are not to be thrown in the trash basket because that will be of no help to any one, we should talk to these people and encourage them. Ladies and gentlemen when we pray and ask God for help, these help are not coming from the skys, God use people to help people.

## I HAVE SEEN MY CROWN WHAT ABOUT YOU?

*It* appears that the Apostle Paul was released from prison after the record of Acts 28. About 64 AD. And that he travelled 5 or 6 years going eastward into macedonia and ASIA minor 1 TIM 1:v3, Tit 3:12 as anticipated in PHIL 1: 26 CH 2: 24, and that he was arrested again and sent to ROME for execution after writing 2 TIM, IN 2 TIM 4: 6-8. Paul said, for I am now ready to be offered, and the time of my departure is at hand. I have fought a good fight, I have finish my course, I have kept the faith. Henceforth there is laid up for me a crown of righteousness, which the righteous judge, shall give me at that day and not for me only, but unto all them also that love his appearing. I don't know if the Apostle Paul had seen his crown, but this we know that he gain the prize v7 and a crown of righteousness is waiting for him.

I have seen my crown many years ago in a night vision, I dream seeing Jesus coming to me riding on a brown horse and he was talking to me, then the horse was lifted up and I was looking at him going up, and I heard him said, O he want to come, so he came back down and grab me around my waist and hold me in his arms like a child, and we were going up. Then just a mind said look over your head, and when I look, there was a beautiful crown, just beautiful. These crowns are not automatic, a person must be faithful to the end, the prize must be won, and we will also receive a crown of righteousness that the righteous judge will give unto us on that day. How could a Christian have dreams of this nature and do not believe that God is communicating with his people in dreams and visions.

## WHY WOULD THE LORD TELL A PREACHER WHAT TO PREACH?

*While* the apostle Paul was at corinth preaching the gospel, Paul evidently became weary of continued fights with the jews there and probably his own life was in danger, so to encourage and comfort him and to prevent him from leaving corinth, the lord made his will clear to the apostle Paul to stay there. IN Acts 18: 9-11, Then spake the Lord in the night by a vision, be not afraid, but speak, and hold not thy peace for I am with thee, and no man shall set on thee to hurt thee, for I have much people in this city and he continued there one year and six months, teaching the word of God among them.

The Lord speak to people today also in similar ways in dreams and visions just as he did with the apostle Paul. Some years ago I was ask to preach at a certain church. That same evening I was lying down having my evening rest, and I heard the voice of the Lord said to me, use a thought that will break a revival. Why would the Lord want me to preach this kind of message? is because the Lord knows the heart of people, he know the ground was fertile and was ready for the seeds to be planted. The Lord know's the needs of the people, so the Lord spoke to me in this vision and told me what to preach not every one will want to believe that the Lord still talk to people today just as he did in the days of the apostle Paul.

TO preach a message to bring about a revival take far more than talking scriptures, it take the anointing power of the Holy Ghost. This kind of message is like a good shower of rain on a dry and thirsty land, the grass will grow again, the flowers will bloom again, the trees will put forth buds and fruits will be on the branches again. The spirit of the Lord will do this, he will revive us. This kind of vision humbled me and let me know that the same Jesus who spoke to the apostle Paul is still working with us today.

I learn that the Lord want us to feed his church with spiritual nutritious food so that his people can grow healthy. The apostle Paul said, Take heed therefore unto yourselves, and to all the flock, over the which the Holy Ghost hath made you overseers, to feed the church of God, which he hath purchased with his own blood.

# A VISION OF PROPHECY

What I am about to tell you will let you say that's impossible, but I must remind you that with God all things are possible. prophecy today is as real as they were in the days of the prophets. some years ago a good friend and brother in the Lord invited me to a week of meeting a church was having. I never went to that church before, I did not know any one from that church-ON our way to the meeting I told him what the preacher was going to preach about, he look at me and ask, how do you know that? I said to him you will see.

He did not know I could know things like that with men these things are impossible, but if the Lord said so there is no power in hell to change it. Man do not have this ability it can only come from above. We went to the meeting, and when the preacher read his text he turn and look at me and said I think you are a prophet. You may ask, how did I know that? that same evening I was lying down having my evening rest, and the Lord spoke to me and told me what the preacher was going to preach about we must learn to believe God, so we can prove to others that the same Jesus who spoke to the apostle Paul still speaks to people today. These revelations are design for the Lord to get the glory out of it. The Lord always talk to people through dreams and visions it is nothing new, the Lord will do so for many reasons.

SO when the Lord speak to you, don't keep quiet about it but speak that which the Lord has revealed. These revelations are design to build faith and confident in the lord, so believe it and don't make yourself a Christian unbeliever.

## A DAY OF FASTING WAS CALLED AND THE LORD RESPONDED

Some years ago a pastor was having some problems with the bishop and the pastor called for a day of fasting. The pastor called me and ask me to attend, so I did. Some men was coming from head quarters from the united states of America that same week to judge the matter. At one point in the fasting we were all at the alter praying and the Lord gave me two visions, the first one is this. I saw a little boy about four years old, he was holding a golden ball under his arms crossing a very busy street, then someone catch him and keep him safe on the other side.

Immediately after that I saw a staircase attach to the church building from the ground half way up the side, then around the back of the building and down to the ground again. ON the other side going down to the ground I saw 2 or 3 men on the staircase going down to the ground, and I heard the voice of the Lord said, holy officers. After we were finish praying I told the pastor that he have nothing to worry about because the Lord was on his side. THE men came from headquarters that same week and judge the matter, they blame the bishop and the pastor get the victory.

This is the interpretation of the vision. The little boy represent innocent, meaning that the pastor was innocent and will be safe, holy officers mean holy men that would speak justice without taking side. And that was exactly what happen, the Lord will defend the innocent. God is no respecter of persons.

## WHAT DOES IT LOOK LIKE IN HEAVEN? I WENT TO HEAVEN

The heaven and heavens are used 718 times in scripture. They mean the air, clouds, sky, expanse, stars, and planet on which God dwells. The word is also used of that which is high GEN 11: 4, DEUT 1:28. in PSALMS 19:v1 David said the heavens declare the glory of God, and the firmament sheweth his handy work.

To explain what it really look like in heaven is beyond how any human mind can grasp, it is just too vast and glorious. what I am about to tell is no way trying to explain heaven, I can only tell you what I have seen and what I heard. IN THE year 2005, one night I dream that I went to heaven and in heaven I saw a very, very large white dome shape building. The building has many gates from which to enter the building. One would go through a gate and walk a little way, then up a few steps and into the building. There are also streets in heaven that leads to the building, I walk on one of them.

I was standing at one of the gate with many others beside myself, but we could not go in, I saw one person dress in white enter the building from the main gate, but at my gate I could not enter the building because a great dragon was sitting in the walkway this dragon could not be approach, that was the most awful and vicious looking creature I have ever seen, but I could see a great deal of the inside of the building from where I was standing because a very large door was open. Inside the building was filled with very small floating lights, these lights was of every color under the sun and more, they look like pepper light but round like small marbles.

There were millions of these floating lights, words cannot describe the beauty of it. God is light and dwelleth in light. So I stand there looking at the inside of the building and I heard a loud voice said, nothing that defile shall enter. Heaven is for the pure and the free and no unclean person will be able to enter. God dwelleth in light and no man can approach him 1 TIM 6;v16. I DID not see the Lord sitting on his throne but I am convinced his throne is among those lights. This was a very glorious vision among many others that I had. I call these visions, visions of glory because no one goes into those atmosphere and want to return, no one.

### A SONG

*W*e read of a place that's called heaven, it's made for the pure and the free. These truths in God's word he hath given, how beautiful heaven must be.

(chorus) How beautiful heaven must be, sweet home of the happy and free. Fair heaven of rest for the weary, how beautiful heaven must be.

## A DREAM ABOUT A FLOCK OF GOATS AND A LION

While I was at a certain church, I dream that I was travelling on a trail one night, on one side of the trail was clear with some tall trees, on the other side of the trail was covered with very thick bush and many goats was feeding on that side. I notice some of the goats had bite wounds on them, I could not understand what was biting the goats that badly, because the wounds was very large, a big piece of their flesh was gone, and the wounds was fresh. So I start to look around under the bush, and there was a lion tied under that heavy bush, so when any of the goats get close to the lion the lion would attack them. The goats was still feeding but I could see that they were hurting. Before I give you the interpretation of the dream, I would like you to listen to this.

Some years ago I had a similar dream to this one and the Lord gave me the interpretation of the dream within the dream, so when I woke from the dream I did not have to wonder what the dream mean because the Lord told me. It was very important for me was to understand that dream, so the Lord told me, just the way he told the prophet Daniel. So I was quick to understand this one. The meaning of the lion and the goats are according to 1 Peter 5:8-9 Be sober, be watchful because your adversary the devil, as a roaring lion, walketh about seeking whom he may devour, whom resist steadfast in the faith, knowing that the same afflictions are accomplished in your brethren that are in the world.

This is the interpretation of the dream. The lion is the devil and the goats represent the people. If we as Christians get too close to the devil, he will hurt us, and that is what is happening to many people in that church. The lion being tied mean that the devil is limited, he do not have any control over us any more, for greater is he that is in us than he that is in the world 1 JOHN 4:v4

## HAVE YOU EVER SEEN THE RAPTURE (I HAVE)

*I* count myself very bless indeed for the Lord to give me a glimpse of what is going to take place on that glorious day when the Lord shall come to take the church out of the world. I wish every Christian could have a glimpse of this glorious sight. It was early one morning I was in a dream looking towards the east, the eastern sky was looking very different from the way it normally look, but I keep looking until I saw a light coming up over the horizon it look as if the sun was rising, the light came up very slowly until it came in full view. The light was not the sun, the light was Jesus of Nazareth the son of God.

Jesus was there in mid air, he was as bright as the sun with all the rays projecting from him just like the sun, and he shouted with a loud voice, and the shout was his own name, he said Jesus, and when he said that as far as I could see people was going up from every corner to meet the Lord in the air. So I can tell you with all certainty that the Apostle Paul was 100 percent right, when he said in 1 THESS 4: 13-18, But I would not have you to be ignorant, brethren,-concerning them which are asleep, that ye sorrow not, even as others which have no hope. v14 For if we believe that Jesus died and rose again even so them also which sleep in Jesus will God bring with him. v15 For this we say unto you by the word of the Lord, that we which are alive and remain unto the coming of the Lord shall not prevent them which are asleep v16 For the Lord himself shall descend from heaven with a shout, with the voice of the archangel, and with the trump of God, and the dead in christ shall rise first. v17 Then we which are alive and remain shall be caught up together with them in the clouds, to meet the Lord in the air, and so shall we ever be with the Lord.v18 wherefore comfort one another with these words.

## A VISION OF JESUS AS BRIGHT AS THE SUN

*I* can also say that John was also 100 percent right, in REV 21:v23 the Apostle John speak of the light of the new Jerusalem, this is what he said. And the city had no need of the sun, neither of the moon, to shine in it, for the glory of God did lighten it, and the lamb is the light thereof, ladies and gentlemen I have seen the Lord for myself and I can tell you that there will be no need for the light of the sun.

For the people who do not believe in dreams please tell me who was I looking at. There will be a literal temple in the new Jerusalem REV 3:v12 said, Him that overcometh will I make a pillar in the temple of my God and he shall go no more out, and I will write upon him the name of my God, which is the new Jerusalem, which cometh down out of heaven from my God: and I will write upon him my new name.

Therefore are they before the throne of God, and serve him day and night in the temple, and he that sitteth on the throne shall dwell among them REV 7: 15) And the temple of God was open in heaven and there was seen in his temple" the ark of his testament, and there were lightenings, and voices, and thunderings, and an earthquake, and great hail REV ll:v19) And another angel came out of the temple, crying with a loud voice to him that sat on the cloud, thrust in thy sickle and reap, for the time is come for thee to reap, for the harvest of earth is ripe. And he that sat on the clouds thrust in his sickle on the earth and the earth was reaped. And another angel came out of the temple which is in heaven, he also having a sharp sickle REV 14:15-17).

REV 15: 1-8, REV 16: v1, v12) The meaning here is simple that men will no longer go to building as the only place to meet with God, as in the earthly temple at Jerusalem, for God and the lamb will be visible pre sent among men to meet with them in all place v3-7 And they sing the song of moses the servant of God, and they song of the lamb, saying great and marvellous are thy works, Lord God almighty, Just and true are thy ways thou king of saints. v4 Who shall not fear thee, o Lord and glorify thy name? for thou only art holy, for all nations shall come and worship before thee, for thy judgment are made manifest. v5 And after that I looked and behold the temple of the tabernacle and the testimony..'-in heaven was open. v6 And the seven angel came out of the temple, having the seven plagues, clothed in pure and white linen, and having their breasts girded with golden girdeles. v7 And one of the four beast gave unto the seven angels seven golden vials full of the wrath of God, who live for ever and ever. v8 And the temple was filled with smoke from the glory of God, and from his power and no man was able to enter the temple, until the seven plagues of the seven angels were fulfilled.

REV 16: 1, And I heard a great voice out of the temple to the seven angels go your way, and pour out the vials of the wrath of God upon the earth. v17) And the seventh angel poured out his vial into the air and there came a great voice out of the temple of heaven, from the throne, saying it is done.

REV 22: 3-5 And there shall be no more curse, but the throne of God and the lamb shall be in it and his servants shall serve him. v4 And they shall see his face and his name shall be in their foreheads. v5 And there shall be no night there and they need no candle, neither light of the sun,f or the Lord God giveth them light, and they shall reign for ever and ever

There will be no more curse that came as a result of lucifer and Adam's rebellion conditions will return back to the way it was before the fall of man, and it will continue that way eternally as if there had never been a curser all rebels will be cast into the lake of fire and serve as a reminder of God's wrath on sin and as a warning to coming generations in all eternity that the wages of sin is death in hell fire-sin does not pay.

The new heaven and earth and the new people will be the same ones we have today only that they will be in a new state-All things will be made new, not new things being made to take the place of the old. It will be a new system, we will not be able to live as we are living today because the former things are past away. REV 21:v5,REV 22:v 3)

The servants will be the faithful angels, redeemed men, and all other creatures that have not rebelled or that have redeemed from all possibility of rebellion in all eternity. (EPH 1: v10, That in the dispensation of the fullness of times he might gather together in one all things in christ, both which are in heaven, and which on the earth. (1 COR 15:24-28 Then cometh the end, when he shall have delivered up the kingdom to God, even the father; when he shall have put down all rules and all authority and power. v25 For he must reign, till he hath put all enemies under his feet. v26 The last enemy that shall be destroyed is death. v27 For he hath put all things under his feet, but when he saith all things are put under him, it is manifest that he is excepted, which did put all things under him. v28 And when all things shall be subdued unto him, then shall the son also himself be subject unto him that put all things under him, that God may be all in all.

At the end of the millennium. This is proved by the fact christ must reign 1000 years to put down all rebellion and then deliver the kingdom to God that he may be all and all as it was before the rebellion. REV 20: 1-10,REV 21: 1-22.GR. TELOS, is not the same end as in REV 1; v8 christ coming brings that end, but this end will not come until 1.000 years later when all rebellion has been put down and the made new (REV 20: 1-10, REV 21: 1-22) THE father is the excepted one, the son and his millennial earthly kingdom do not cease to exist for both are eternal.

The son will continue to reign under the father after the earth is rid of all rebellion. ISAIAH 9:6-7 For unto us a child is born, unto us a son is given, and the government shall be upon his shoulders: and his name shall be called wonderful, counselor, the mighty God, the everlasting father the prince of peace. of the increase of his government of peace there shall be no end, upon the throne of David and upon his kingdom, to order it, and to establish it with-judgment and with justice from henceforth even for ever. The zeal of the Lord of hosts will perform this.

## A VISION ON A COMMUNION SUNDAY

*It* was on a beautiful sunday morning, we all gathered for worship, the pastor was speaking, the communion table was set. I was sitting at the end of the bench close to isles, and I saw a small beautiful lady coming up the isles before me, she was carrying both communion vessels, one in the right and the other in the left, I looked at her for about 4 or 5 seconds. I touch the lady that was sitting before me on the shoulder, and ask her if she believe in visions, she said yes I do, so I told her the vision that I had. She ask what does it mean? so I told her that the Lord wanted us to know that he is with us. The Lord is confirming to us that we are doing the right thing. The Lord was not saying to serve the Lord SUPPER the way I saw it, no, it was only a confirmation.

The Lord supper was reveal to Paul by revelation. GAL 1: v12, FOR I neither received it of man, neither was I taught it, but by revelation of Jesus christ. How that by revelation he made known unto me the mystery,(as I wrote afore in few words.

1 CORIN 11: 23-26 For I have received of the Lord that which also I delivered unto you, that the Lord Jesus the same night in which he was betrayed took bread. v24 And when he had given thanks, he break it, and said, take eat, this is my body, which is broken for you, this do in remembrance of me. v25 After the same manner also he took the cup, when he had supped, saying, this cup is the new testament in my blood, this do ye as oft as ye drink it, in remembrance of me. v26 For as often as ye eat this bread, and drink this cup, ye do show the Lord's death till he come.

After he comes it will be observed in the kingdom. Luke 22:16-20 v30 matt 26:v29 (it symbolizes his blood that seals the new covenant which based upon better promises. HEB 8:v6 (But now hath he obtained a more excellent ministry, by how much also he is the mediator of a better covenant, which was established upon better promises.

Heb 9:15-22. For if these carnal rites and ceremonies set the body apart and ceremonially purify the flesh of defilement giving it re-admission to public worship and freedom from temporal punishment of the law, how much more shall the blood of christ, through the holy spirit purge your conscience from sin and make you inwardly holy before God.

The rituals of the law only cleansed the body-the flesh (v13) but the blood of Christ cleanses the soul and spirit and reconcile us to God, or bring one back into fellowship with God, v 14-15) COL 1:14-22 IN whom we have redemption through his blood, even the forgiveness of sins. v15 Who is the image of the invisible God, the firstborn of every creature: v16 For by him were all things created, that are in heaven, and that are in earth, visible and invisible, whether they be thorns or dominions, principalities, or powers; all things were created by him and for him. v17 And he is before all things, and by him all things consist. v18 And he is the head of the body, the church, who is the beginning, the firstborn from the dead; that in all things he might have pre-eminence. v19 For it pleased the father that in him should all fullness dwell. v20 And having made peace through the blood of his cross, by him to reconcile all things unto himself: by him, I say, whether they by things in the earth, or in heaven,.

v2l And you, that were some time alienated and enemies in your mind by wicked works, yet now hath he reconciled.(or bring back into fellowship with God.) v22 IN the body of his flesh through death; to present you holy and unblameable and unreproveable in his sight.

The person we now know as Jesus christ, the only begotten son of God, existed as an equal member of the Godhead from the beginning ISA 7:v14,CH 9: 6-7,MIC 5: v2, John 1:v1-2,HEB 1: v8,REV 1: v 8-11. before Jesus became God's son(sonship refers to humanity, not deity, ACts 13: 33) he was a spirit being and carried out the divine plan of creation with the father. He was directly from God the father who created all things by him. This proves that the heavens and the things are just as material as those on earth v16. GEN 1:v1, prov 8:27 When he prepared the heavens, I was there, when he set a compass upon the face of the depth.

invisible things are made up of material substance which is visible in its own realm. created things, including spirit beings such as angels, cherubim, seraphim, etc, all are of material substance but some substance are higher type than others. Though all are visible in their own realms, some may not be visible in other realms that are of a lower substance. spirit being are of a higher substance than flesh and blood because we are of ordinary material that we see.

Those that are of higher substance are not limited to ordinary substance as we know it. because they can go through closed doors, walls, and other material objects, as proved by what is recorded in scripture of angels and others, even the material, spiritual, and immortalized body of christ, a real flesh and bone body. LUKE 24:v39) can go through material walls without an opening (JOHN 20: v19 LUKE 24: 31,35-43. IF this is true of angels and resurrected human bodies, could it not be true of God the father and the holy spirit.

## A VISION OF 2-MEN STANDING IN MID AIR

*I* can assure you that each time we gathered together for worship we are not alone, It was on a beautiful sunday morning we gather for worship, church was full and the preacher was preaching and straight before were 2 men standing in mid air about 30 feet from me. I said to a young man that was sitting beside me, the Lord is in this place, so I told him the vision, he looked but saw nothing. I believe that the Lord are revealing these things to his people all over the world but we are not hearing about them. I know those 2 men were the angels of the Lord. Angels are spirit beings and are with God's people where ever we go. PSALM 34:v7 The angel of the Lord encampeth round about them that fear him, delivereth them.

## SALVATION

*B*ecause of salvation the Lord allow us to see and know things we could not know, because we were in darkness, we live in darkness, and walk in darkness. ISAIAH 9:v2 said, The people that walked in darkness have seen a great light: they that dwell in the land of the shadow of death, upon them hath the light shined. And the light shineth in darkness and the darkness comprehended it not JOHN 1: v5.

## WHAT IS SALVATION

*T*he Hebrew word is yeshu-ah the Greek word are, so-terion) in the Bible the word" salvation is not nessarily a technical theological term but simply mean" deliverance from almost any kind of evil, whether material or spiritual. Theologically, however, it denotes (1) the whole process by which man is delivered from all that interferes with the enjoyment of God's highest blessings, (2) the actual enjoyment of those blessings. The root idea in salvation is deliverance from, some danger or evil. This deliverance may be from defeat in battle EXOD 15:v2 The Lord is my strength and song, and he is become my salvation: he is my God," and I will prepare him an habitation, my father's God, and I will exalt him. PSALM 34:v6 This poor man cried, and the Lord heard him, and saved him out of all his troubles.

2 SAMUEL 22:v3 The God of my rock, in him will I trust, he is my shield, and the horn of my salvation, my high tower, and my refuge, my saviour, thou savest me from violence. PSALM 57: v3 He shall send from heaven and save me from the reproach of him that would swallow me up. God shall send forth his mercy and his truth. PSALM 6:v4 Return o Lord, deliver my soul: oh save

me for thy mercies sake.

EZEKIEL 36:v29) I will also save you from all your uncleannesses: and I will call for the corn, and I will increase it, and lay no famine upon you. The outstanding instance of divine salvation is in the early history of Israel was the deliverance from EGYP,t,. Since it is God who provide the deliverance, he is often spoken of as saviour ISAIAH 43:11, For I am the Lord thy God, the holy one of Israel, thy saviour: I gave EGYPT for thy ransom, Ethiopia and seba for thee: vll,I even I am the Lord; and beside me there is no saviour.

JER 14:v8 is a title which in the New Testament is usually applied to Jesus christ. in the old testament salvation is at first thought of as deliverance from present evil in a temporal and material sense. but with depending sense of moral evil, salvation acquires a profound ethical meaning.

At first the concept of salvation is primarily national but gradually the prophetic horizon broadens and salvation is seen to include gentiles as well as Jews ISAIAH 49:v5-6) CH 55:1-5. There is also increasing stress upon individual Salvation is not necessarily for the nation on a whole, but for the righteous remnant, it includes moreover, deliverance from sin itself as well as from the various evils which are the consequence of sin PSALM 51:, JER 31:31-34, EZEK 36:25-29. with the development of the messianic idea the word salvation comes to be used in the technical theological sense of the deliverance, especially from sin, to be brought in with the messianic age.

IN the Old testament complete trust in God was the most important of the human conditions for salvation. Next in importance, and following naturally from the first, was obedience to God's moral law as expressed in the various codes of the law, God, however, was not satisfied with a mere legalistic fulfillment of the letter of the law. Forgiveness of sin was conditioned upon repentance. Most sins also required a ritual sacrifice as part of the act for repentance.

IN the teaching of Jesus, salvation is often used to mean

✧ ✧ ✧ ✧ ✧ ✧ ✧ ✧ ✧ ✧ ✧ ✧ ✧ ✧ ✧ ✧ ✧ ✧

deliverance from trouble, like illness Matt 9: v22) But Jesus turned him about, and when saw her, he said, daughter, be of good comfort, thy faith hath made thee whole, And the woman was made whole from that hour. But it usually means deliverance from sin through entrance upon a new divine life. It is a present experience, although its complete fulfillment Is eschatological. To the pharisees of his day, salvation was a reward given to the man who perfectly live up to the requirement of the law; but Jesus say that he come to seek and to save that which was lost. LUKE 19:v10)and that salvation is through faith in him, the incarnate son of God, JOHN 3: v16)

THE central theme of the entire apostolic age is the salvation that is brought by Jesus christ. salvation is represented primarily as deliverance from sin. The whole New Testament lays stress upon the sufferings and death of christ as mediating salvation (EPH 2:13-18 But now in christ Jesus ye who sometimes were far off are made nigh by the blood of christ. v14 For he is our peace, who hath made both one, and hath broken down the middle wall of partition between us.

V15 Having abolished in his flesh the enmity, even the law of commandment contained in ordinances, for to make in himself of twain one new man, so making peace. v16 And that he might reconcile both unto God in one body by the cross, having slain the enmity thereby. v17 And came and preach peace to you which were afar off, and to them that were nigh. v 18 For through him we both have access by one spirit unto the father.

AS in the teaching of Jesus, salvation throughout the new testament is regarded as a present experience, but it is eschatological as well indeed, the blessings of salvation the believer has now are only a foretaste of what it is going to be in the coming age, after christ comes. The salvation christ brings is not merely deliverance from "future punishment, but also from sin which is a present power ROM 6: 1-2 What shall we say then? shall we continue in sin, that grace may abound? God forbid. How shall we, that are dead to sin, live any longer therein.

❖ ❖ ❖ ❖ ❖ ❖ ❖ ❖ ❖ ❖ ❖ ❖ ❖ ❖ ❖ ❖ ❖ ❖

It includes all the redemptive blessings we have in christ, chiefly conversion, regeneration, Justification, adoption, sanctification,and glorification. It provides a solution for the whole problem of sin, in all its many aspects. Through union with christ, the believer is now dead to sin ROM 6: v2 we crucified the flesh or corrupt human nature GAL 5:v24 And they that are christ's have crucified the flesh with the affections and lusts.

We has become a new creature 2 COR 5: v17 Therefore if any man be in christ he is a new creature, old things are passed away behold, all things are become new. we are free from the law ROM 6:v14 (For sin shall not have dominion over you, for ye are not under the law, but under grace. CH7':v6 But now we are delivered from the law, that being dead wherein we were held, that we should serve in the newness of spirit and not in the oldness of the letter. And has exchanged the bondage of its requirement for THE freedom of the new man in christ (COL 2:v14 Blotting out the hand writing of ordinances that was against us, which was contrary to us, and took it out of the way, nailing it to his cross: GAL 5: v1 (Stand fast therefore in the liberty wherewith, christ hath made us free, and be not entangled again in the yoke of bondage.

v13 For, brethren ye have been called unto liberty, only use not liberty for an occasion to the flesh, by love serve one another v18 but if ye be led by the spirit, ye are not under the law. The reception of deliverance is made possible by faith, which is not mere mental compliance to certain doctrinal propositions, but repentance and whole hearted commitment to christ as saviour and Lord(ROM 3:v28) Therefore we conclude that a man is sanctified BY faith without the deeds of the law (EPH 2:v8 For by grace are ye saved through faith, and not of yourselves, it is the gift of God.

ON the divine side, the ultimate cause of salvation is the divine mercy of God. It is entirely undeserved, and is by God's grace alone. SO far as receiving God's grace is concerned, salvation is available to all people every where(JOHN 3:16) For God so love,, the world that he gave his only begotten son that whosoever believeth in him should not perish but have everlasting life.

1 TIM 4: v10, IN some sense, the doctrine of salvation extends beyond man so as to affect the universe. Eventually all things will be subjected unto the son (1 COR 15:v28) And when all things shall be subdued unto him, then shall the son also himself be subject unto him that put all things under him, that God may be all in all. And all things in heaven and on earth will be summed up in christ (EPH 1:v10) That in the dispensation of the fullness of times he might gather together in one all things in christ, both which are in heaven, and which are on earth, even in him. NO foe will remain to dispute christ authority or in way to mar the glories of his eternal kingdom. Even the physical universe will be redeemed.

## MY FIRST VISION OF PROPHECY ABOUT A FLYING CAR

It was in the year 1965, 1 was a young Christian in my home church, then one night in a vision I saw a flying car, and the man that pilot the car looked out the window and looked at me because the car was about 60 or 70 feet above the earth. At that time I did not know what to make of the vision because I had no knowledge of what a flying car was all about. IN 1989 the Lord gave me the vision again for the second time of this flying car.

By now I grow in knowledge and understand that the Lord was showing a future aircraft. Whenever a dream or a vision re-peat itself it is a conformation telling you that the dream or vision is true. Today it is not a dream any more but a reality. I was watching tv one day many years later and I heard them talking about this flying car, and that some body have the prototype of this flying car. They called it sky car. Dreams and visions inform us of future advents that we cannot know on our own, we do not have this ability. So look for this flying car it is coming.

## A PROPHECY ABOUT WHAT IS GOING TO HAPPEN IN SPACE

*I*t was in the year 1965 the Lord gave me this vision of prophecy about space. IN the dream I saw a highway started from the earth and reaches all the way into space, it was gone beyond sight. ON the highway up there, there were men engaged in a vicious sword fight many miles above the earth. that fight will take place in the future. At that time I did not know any thing about space until many years later, then I understood that the Lord showed me the exploration of space you may ask, why would they fight? I don't know, but I believe they are going to find something that will be of great prize and they will fight over it. They will not fight for nothing.

Lately these days I heard the united states of America talking about putting weapon in space, when ever they do ' it will not for show they will use them. This will take place in the future.

## A PROPHECY ABOUT A PLANET THAT WILL BE OCCUPIED BY HUMANS

*I*t was in the early 1980's the Lord took me to a planet in a night vision the planet was a mighty long way from earth it appears I was flying all night, when I reach the planet and landed on the ground I look back to see where I came from and it was total darkness, but on the planet itself was beautiful daylight. I realize I was far above the earth. The only way I can describe the planet is to say it is a vast desert, and also look like earth, only that there were no trees, grass, or water, only stones, and large rocks, just the way they are on earth. I saw hundreds of people there, they were living in tent like structures and they were not aliens, I said they were not aliens. They were there on vacation having a good time and they were humans just like you and I. The atmosphere was like the west Indian Islands, I do not believe it will be colonized, because there were no trees, grass, or water.

## ABOUT SIX MONTHS LATER

*I* said this before and I am saying it again when ever a dream or vision repeat itself it is a conformation that the dream or vision is true. About six months after the first vision, I had a second dream, but this time I was telling a large crowed of people about the first vision I had in going to this planet. After I was finish talking to the people there was a tall handsome young man that was standing in front of the crowed, said, I gave you that vision (that was the Lord) then I heard a voice, said, go, that mean I should go and prophesy. As sure as night follows the day this vision will come to pass. So tell your children and grand children about it.

## LETS TALK ABOUT PROPHETS

*W*ho is a prophet? there are Hebrew words that are used in the old testament to designate the prophets, namely, navi, RA-eh, and hozeh. The last two are participles, and may be rendered" seer. They are practically meaning the same thing. The first term, navi,is difficult to explain or the origin of the word although various attempts have been made. The significance of these words, however, may be learned from their usage.

Each of these words designates one who is a spokesman for God. The usage of navi is illustrated in EXODUS 4: 15-16 And thou shall speak unto him. And put words in his mouth and I will be with thy mouth, and with his mouth, and will teach you what ye shall do. v16 And he shall be spokesman unto the people and he shall be, even he even he shall be to thee instead of a mouth, and thou shalt be to him instead of God. CH 7: v1 And the Lord said unto moses, see, I have made thee a God to pharaoh: and Aaron thy brother shall be thy prophet.

IN these passages it is clearly taught that moses stands in relation to the pharaoh as God. Between them is an intermediary, Aaron, Aaron stand between pharaoh and Moses, and speak to pharaoh the words which Moses gave him. SO a prophet is one who speak forth for God.

The two words ro-eh, and hozeh, perhaps have primary reference to the fact that the person so designated see the message which God give to him. This seeing probably to be conceived as having taken place in a vision. At the same time, even these two words serve to designate a man who, having seen the message of the Lord, and declares that message. The Biblical emphasis throughout is practical. It is not the dark background of the method of reception of the prophetic revelation that stands in front but the deliverance of the message of God.

The prophet of the Greeks are not the same as the prophet of the Lord so they must be distinguished one from the other. The prophets of the Greeks acted as interpreters for the muses and oracles. The prophet of the Lord, however, were not interpreters. They uttered the actual words which the Lord had given to them, without any modification or interpretation on their part.

The Bible itself gives an accurate description of the function of the true prophet. DEUT 18:v18, I will raise them up a prophet from among their brethren, like unto thee, and I will put my words in his mouth; and he shall speak unto them all that I have command him v19, And it shall come to pass, that whosoever will not hearken unto my words which he shall in my name, I will require it of him.

All prophecy is not of God, nor be the name and inspiration of God. Prophecy that is supposed to be in the name of the Lord may or may not be of him. A mere claim is no proof. If the prophecy come to pass it is generally accepted as from God, however, this test is not absolute, because in DEUT 13:v 1-3,the word of God stated that he may allow a sign or wonder (spoken by a false prophet) to come to prove his people and see if they will act contrary to his own words. Therefore, the real test is not only to see whether a prophecy come to pass or not but also to see if it is in harmony with the word of God. This is the final and complete test. Anything contrary to the word of God is false, because God will never contradict himself.

## A PROPHECY FULFILLED IN THE CHURCH

*I*N 1972 1 was worshiping at a certain church, then one night in a vision I saw a lady preacher, and she was preaching and said, the Lord shall raise up one from among you. So I prophesy and said thus saith the Lord of host, I shall raise up one from among you. Every one in the church heard what I said. About two weeks after the prophecy, it happen. we gather for worship one sunday evening, and while the service was in progress the Holy spirit took hold of a young brother in a way that I have not seen before. He was slain in the spirit, and filled with the Holy spirit, lying on the floor speaking with other tongues and praising God just the way it was on the day of pentecost. The Lord honour his word he did what he said he would do, he raise him up just as he said.

This brother was a very faithful brother in the church for years but he was not filled with the Holy spirit until that glorious night, he was now filled with the Holy Ghost and fire, the anointing power of the Holy Ghost now rest on his life. This brother went off to Bible school for a few years, then came back and pastor church for many years, then became the superintendent for the churches in canada. The Lord will do what he said he would do.

Any one who claim to be a Christian and do not believe that prophecy is a real Christian experience in the church today, I would love to have a chat with them. For one to prophesy you must hear the voice of the Lord who tells you what to say, or you see what he want you to prophesy about. Any other prophecy is false.

## DO NOT FORGET TO PRAY

*P*rayer is of great value, it is as important as air water and food to keep us alive. people every where seek favour and relationship with that higher power regardless what their understanding maybe people never outgrow the need for prayer. Living in a world of uncertainty surrounded by the vast and terrifying forces of nature, the inescapable shadow of death, people in their weakness, anguish, and need, people need to pray, some will pray for the first time especially in times of crisis then the true nature of prayer is revealed, PSALMS 107:23-28.)

The Bible teaches us also how the priests of Baal cried unto their Gods, without any answer 1 KINGS 18:v 26-29) also the idolators of Anthena, Paul found their alters every where Acts 17: 15-23) people have the need to get in touch with God who hears and answer prayer. David said, o thou that hearest prayer, unto thee shall all flesh come, PSALMS 65:v2) prayer keep us in communication with God, prayer is the well spring for the Christian life.

IF a Christian to neglect praying means that such a person will be living on a dry and thirsty land. some things will not happen without prayer, Jesus said men should always pray and not to faint LUKE 18:v1, Jesus also said, Ask and it shall be given you; seek, and ye shall find, knock, and it shall be open unto you. For every one that asketh receiveth, and that seeketh findeth; and to him that knocketh it shall be opened. Or what man is there of you, whom if his son ask bread, will he give him a stone. or if he ask a fish, will he give him a serpent? IF ye then, being evil, know how to give good gifts unto your children, how much more shall your father which is in heaven give good things to them that ask him? Matt 7: 7-11.

## CHRISTIANS ARE NOT TO WORRY, BELIEVERS ARE WARNED NOT TO TRUST IN RICHES

*M*att 6: 19-21 Jesus said, Lay not up for yourselves treasures upon earth, where moth and rust doth, corrupt, and where thieves break through and steal. v20 But lay up for yourselves treasures in heaven, where neither moth nor rust doth corrupt, and where thieves do not break through and steal. v21 For where your treasure is, there will your heart be also. Eastern treasures were of find clothes, polished armour, weapons of war, Gold, and jewels, moth and rust were as destructive to most of them as thieves. To lay up treasures in heaven is to consecrate yourself fully to the Lord Jesus christ and to help those that are in need. Even a simple cup of cold water given given in the right spirit will be rewarded Matt 10:40-42.

Mansions and furnishings in heaven are secure from moths and termites, metals are free from rust, precious stones are free from thieves, and all hearts are safe from fear or loss forever. (Reasons for the advice of COL 3: 1-4) IF ye then be risen with christ, seek those things which are above, where christ sitteth on the right hand of God. v2 Set your affections on things above, not things on the earth. v3 For ye are dead, and your life is hid with christ in God. v4 Where christ who is our life, shall appear, then shall ye also appear with him in glory. Do not worry or over-anxious or fretful. many people will not marry because they have not seen the material things, so they will have to take their love elsewhere. Such a person are telling me that their affections are not on things above, but on things on earth.

## (8) REASONS WHY WE SHOULD NOT WORRY

Life is more than meat, the body is more than raiment, men are greater than material things, men are greater than the fowls whom God feeds without their labour.

Worry cannot change the body into what you want it to be, men are better than plants they do not worry about clothing, The providence of God is over all creation, he provide for all. worry is useless and sinful, do not let it be a part of the Christian experience because it not. worry do not make life better, it make it worst. because of worry many are sick. worrying is not good, it will injure your soul. God alone can help you, and he will do it if you will pray about every thing that happens and give thanks for everything. PHIL 4:v6-7 (The apostle Paul said) Be-careful for nothing;

but in every thing by prayer and supplication with thanksgiving let your request be made known unto God. v7 And the peace of God, which passeth all understanding, shall keep your hearts and minds through christ Jesus. 1 THESS 5: v18 IN every thing give thanks, for this is the will of God in christ Jesus concerning you.

## THE PARABLE OF THE RICH FOOL

The parable of the rich man should be a lesson for us all, but are we learning any thing? many people are selling their soul to get riches, this is madness and are not to be found among Christians.

IN LUKE 12-: 16-21(Jesus speak a parable about a rich man, saying, The ground of a certain rich man brought forth plentifully. v17 And he thought within himself, saying, what shall I do, because I have no room where to bestow my fruits? v18 And he said this will I do, I will pull down my barns, and build a. "greater one, and there I will bestow all my fruits and my goods. v19 And I will say to my soul, soul,t hou hast much goods laid up for many years; take thine ease, eat, drink, and be merry. v20 But God said unto him, thou fool, this night shall thy soul be, required of thee, then whose shall those thing's , be, which thou hast provided?. v2l,So is he that layeth up treasures for himself, and is not rich toward God.

This parable teaches us that we should make more provisions for the soul than the body. never seek riches at the expense of the soul welfare, we learn that we are not to waste our life to get riches, put important things first. Laying up treasures only on earth will damn the soul.

## RICHES CAN CREATE PRIDE

Too many people do not take the time to learn how to handle riches., it is nice to be rich so one can be very independent. you can buy whatever you need, you can go where ever you want, you can help your family and those that are in need, but at the same time danger stands at the door because riches create tools that the devil use to destroy many and pierce themselves through with many sorrows.

Riches cause many temptations of the devil
riches cause many snares of the devil
riches cause many foolish lusts
riches cause many harmful lusts
riches cause destruction and spiritual ruin
riches cause the root of evil to grow
riches cause people to err from the faith
riches is the cause of many sorrows
riches cause many to be. highminded, proud and boastful, riches in scripture, are considered to be the cause of much sin and rebellion against God. And for this cause there are many warnings to men, especially converted men, to shun all covetousness of such. not all men love money that much to cause them to fall.

The very thing that they coveted after has now become an enemy to the soul. (TIM 6: 6-10) But Godliness with contentment is great gain. v7 For we brought nothing into this world, and it is certain we can carry nothing out. v8 And having food and raiment let us be therewith content. v9 But they that will be rich fall into temptation and a snare, and into many foolish and hurtful lusts, which drawn men into destruction and perdition. v10, For the love of money is the root of all evil; which while some coveted after, they have erred from the faith, and pierced themselves through with many sorrows.

v17-19, Charge them that are rich in this world, that they be not highminded, nor trust in uncertain riches, but in the living God, who giveth to us richly all things to enjoy. v18, That they do good, that they be rich in good works, ready to distribute, willing communicate. v19 Laying up in store for themselves a good foundation against the time to come, that they may lay hold on eternal life.

## A SONG I AM A CHILD OF A KING

*My* father is rich in houses and land, he holdeth the wealth of the world in his hands of rubies, and diamond, and silver and gold, His coffers are full, he have riches untold. CHORUS) I am a child of a king, l am a child of a king with Jesus my saviour I am a child of a king.

(2) MY fathers own son the saviour of men, once wonder oer earth as the poorest of them, but now he is reigning forever on high and will give me a home in heaven by and by.

(3) I once was a outcast stranger on earth, a sinner by choice, and a alien by birth, but I've been adapted, my name is written down, an heir of a mansion a robe and a crown.

(4) A tent or a cottage why should I care, they are building a place for me over there, tho exiled from home, yet still I may sing, all glory to God, I am a child of a king.

## WHAT IS LIFE

*Life* is a complex concept with varied shades of meaning, rendering several HEB, and GR, Terms, it may mean physical or natural life, whether animal, it is the vital principle, or breath of life, which God breathed into man, making him a living soul GEN 2:v7) And the Lord God formed man of the dust of the ground. and breathed into his nostrils the breath of life; and man became a living soul. Life is a precious gift and the taking of life is prohibited GEN 9:v5, EXOD 20: v13, thou shalt not kill. LEV 24:v17 and he that killeth any man shall surely be put to death. It is propagated through physical generation and it is subject to physical death. It may signify the period of one's earthly existence, one's lifetime or the relations, activities, and experiences which make up life, EXOD 1: v14, DEUT 32:v47,JOB 10:v1, LUKE 12:v15, occasionally it means one's manner of life, 1 TIM 2: 2-3 For kings, and for all that are in authority, that we may lead a quiet and peaceable life in all godliness and honesty. v3 For this is good and acceptable in the sight of God our saviour. 1 John 2:v16, For all that is in the world, the lust of the flesh. and the lust of the eye, and the pride of life, is not of the father. but is of the world. or the means of sustaining life, (DEUT 24:v6,) 1 JOHN 3:v17) but the primary concern of the scriptures is spiritual or eternal life for man.

Life is the gift of God, mediated through faith in Jesus christ, John 3:v36 He that believeth on the son hath everlasting life, and he that believeth not shall not see life, but the wrath of God abideth on him, (CH 5:24 verily, verily, I say unto you, He that heareth my words and believeth on him that sent me hath ever-lasting life, and shall not come into condemnation but is pass from death unto life. ROMANS 5:v10 For if, when we were enemies we were reconciled to God by the death of his son much more, being reconciled, we shall be saved by his life.

CH 6:v23, For the wages of sin is death, but the gift of God is eternal life through Jesus christ our Lord. 1 John 5:v12 etc HE that hath the son hath life, and he that hath not the son of God hath not life. It is synonymous with endless existence, which is also true with the unsaved, it is (qualitative) depending on, involv-ing the-impartation of a new nature (2 Peter I:v3-4 According as his divine power hath given unto us all things pertain unto life and Godliness, through the knowledge of him that hath called us to glory and virtue.

v4 Whereby are given-unto us exceeding great and precious promises, that by these ye might be partakers of the divine nature, having escaped the corruption that is in the world through lust. It is communicated to the believer in this life, resulting in fellow-ship with God in christ, and is not interrupted by physical death

(1 THESS 5: v10) Who died for us, that whether we wake or sleep, we should live together with him.

It will find its perfection and full reality of blessedness with God in the life to come. ROMANS 2:v7 To them who by patient continuance in well doing seek for glory and honour and immortality, eternal life. 2 COR 5: v4 For we who are in this tabernacle do groan, being burdened, not for that we would be unclothed, but clothed upon,t hat mortality might be swallowed up of life. (DEUT 5:v26,For who is there of all flesh, that hath heard the voice of the living God speaking out of the midst of the fire, as we have,and lived? PSALM 42:v2 MY soul thirstest for God, for the living God, when shall I come and appear before God?1 thess 1:v9) 2 tim 3:v15) And that from a child thou hast known the holy scriptures, which able make thee wise unto salvation through faith which is in christ Jesus.

The eternal and self existent one. God has absolute life in himself, John 5:26, For as the father hath life in himself, so hath he given to the son to hath life in himself. And is the source of all life. PSALM 36: v9 For with thee is the fountain of life, in thy light shall we see light. John 1:v4 IN him was life, and the life was the light of men. CH 17: v3 And this is life eternal, that they might know thee the only true God, and Jesus christ whom thou hast sent. All scripture centers around the idea of knowing God and of conforming to his eternal will. ignorance of the Lord and refusal to know and to believe in him are condemned many times-in scripture. this is what will damn the soul.

(John 1:1-2) That which was from the beginning, which we have heard, which we have seen with our eyes, which we have looked upon, and our hands have handled, of the word of life. v2 For the life was manifested, and we have seen it, and bear witness, and shew unto you that eternal life, which was with the father, and was manifested unto us. CH 5:v13 These things have I written unto you that believe on the name of the son of God, that ye may know that ye have eternal life, and that ye may believe on the name of the son of God. Some church group teaches that once you are saved you cannot be lost, but such teaching is false. sin is a killer, we are saved from sin, not save to sin, so if a child of God practice sin you will be back where you once were, and the wages of sin is death. ROMANS 6:v23.

2 Peter 1:1-10. This proves that one can have the graces and experiences of v3-7 and then lose them even to the point of actually forgetting he was purged from his old sins v8-9) Peter exhorts every one to be diligent,(careful-watchful) making his calling and election sure, declaring that they who do the things of v4-7 will never fall v10.) why this warning so there be no possibility of one failing to make his calling and election sure.

The second time in 6 verses Christians are warned to give diligence to meeting certain terms of the Lord lest they fall into sin and be lost v5-10) IF you do these things you will never fall v10. Does this not clearly show that if you do not do these things you will fall?.If one fall,what will happen? will his calling and election still sure? will you be still ready to hear well done good and faithful servant? For if God spared not the natural branches, take heed lest ye also will not be spared. ROMANS ll:v2l. The natural branches is ISRAEL and they were not spared, so what about us the wild olive tree? (the gentiles).

## WHAT IS GOD'S WILL

*I*t is God's will that all men would be saved and enjoy all the blessings and promises that are provided through our Lord and saviour Jesus christ, the son of God. Peter said the Lord is not slack concerning his promise, as some men count slackness, but is long suffering to us ward, not willing that any should perish, but that all should come to repentance. 2 Peter 3:v9. We have seen through out the scriptures that it is the will of God for his children is that they get from him and his abundant supply that is needed in this life as well as the one to come. God love his own children infinitely more than we humans love our children, the Lord will give to his children all the good things of life, and that his promises cover every known need of man for body, soul, and spirit for ever, and that his work in providing these benefits is already completed; and all that stands between any man and these promises is his own failure to take the necessary revealed steps in getting them for himself.

## IT IS GOD'S WILL THAT WE PROSPER IN WHAT EVER WE DO

When Joshua take over after the death of Moses, the Lord told Joshua, Be strong and of good courage; for unto this people shalt thou divide for an inheritance the land, which I swore unto their fathers to give them. Only be thou strong and be very courageous; that thou mayest observe to do according to all the law, which Moses my servant commanded thee; turn not from it to the right hand or to the left, that thou mayest prosper whither soever thou goest JOSHUA 1: 6-7.)

It is God's will for his children to be like a tree planted by the rivers water, that bringeth forth his fruit in his season, his leaf also shall not wither, and what soever he doeth shall prosper PSALMS 1:v3). Beloved, I wish above all things that thou mayest prosper and be in health, even as thy soul prospereth. 3 JOHN V2.)

## YOU HAVE A PART TO DO

Remember you have to do in order to attaining to the benefits which christ died. The plan is simple, the will of God is revealed and made plain, you are not in ignorance of what to do, and you should recognize mentally that there is no excuse for any failure if one will obey the truth. This is all right as far as it goes but there must be the definite action on your part. you must be more than give mental consent to the truth. you must act upon it with all your heart, soul, and strength and take the necessary steps before you can experience what you want.

## WHAT IS THE BAPTISM OF THE HOLY SPIRIT?

The spirit baptism is the immersion or burial of the believer in the spirit at which time he receives the spirit in his life in all fullness and without measure, and is endued with power from on high, to do the work of christ Luke 24: v49, John 7:v37-39, CH14: v12-17, Acts 1:4-8, Acts 3:v6, CH 5: 12-16, CH 19:vll, Mark 16: v16-20, Heb 2:v3-4, etc). It is the same full anointing of the spirit that Jesus received ISAIAH 11: 1-2, CH 42: 1-7, CH 61:v1, Matt 11: 4-6, CH 12: v18, CH 20: 22-23, Luke 4:16-21, John 3: v34, CH 14: v12, Acts 10:v38. It is the spirit coming in, upon the believer, filling him with overwhelming, infusing, anointing, and enduing with full power, and not with just a measure, as in the old testament days. It is the Holy spirit taking full possession of the believer to live, speak, and work through him in the same degree that was manifested through christ and the apostles.

## WHY BELIEVERS NEED THE BAPTISM OF THE HOLY SPIRIT

The purpose of the baptism of the holy spirit is not to save the the soul, sanctify one, or make him a child of God, or to qualify one to go in the rapture. Such doctrines are unscriptual as proved by the following. All the old testament saints and the disciples before pentecost were saved, sanctified, justified, and free from all sin. Since they never were baptized in the holy spirit, so the purpose of the baptism of the holy spirit was not to give them these blessings.

Jesus was always sinless, yet he needed the baptism of the holy spirit in order to have power to do his mighty works. The purpose of the baptism of the holy spirit in his case then was not to sanctify him, to save his soul, or to make him a child of God. there are many scriptures which proves that men received the spirit in a measure at the new birth and that these blessings are not the baptism of the holy spirit. The baptism of the holy spirit was promise only to saved men and women after they had repented, and and baptized in water, and were obedient to God, and had ask the Lord for this baptism as a child of god. Matt 3:11, John 1:31-34, CH 14:12-17, v26, CH 15:v26, CH 16:13-15, Acts 1:4-8, CH 2:38-39, CH 5z v32, Luke 11:7-13)

The baptism of the holy spirit was given only to saved men. The disciples were saved and sanctified before receiving the baptism of the holy spirit at pentecost, the samaritans were saved, sanctified, baptized in water, healed and had great joy before Peter and John laid hands on them so they could receive the baptism of the holy spirit Acts 8:5-20.The disciples of John were saved, sanctified, and baptized in water years before Paul laid hands on them so they could receive the baptism of the holy spirit Acts 19:1-7). How could any one read these scriptures and believe with a clear conscience that the new birth is the baptism of the holy spirit.

The only two cases recorded of men receiving the baptism of the holy spirit at the same time they were saved are Paul and the gentiles Acts 9:v17, Acts 22:v16, Acts 10:v43-48, CH ll:v14-18, CH 15:7-11) IN both of these cases they were granted repentance unto life" and their heart were purified by faith" or they could not have received the baptism of the holy spirit. so the purpose of this baptism was not to give them these blessings. The baptism of the holy spirit is not given to qualify the saints to go in the rapture. There are no scripture that said that, that the baptism of the holy spirit is given to qualify Christians for the rapture. The old testament saints will be going into the rapture and they never heard of the baptism of the holy spirit.

◇ ◇ ◇ ◇ ◇ ◇ ◇ ◇ ◇ ◇ ◇ ◇ ◇ ◇ ◇ ◇ ◇ ◇

## WHAT QUALIFY A PERSON FOR THE RAPTURE

$\mathcal{A}$ person must be in christ, which means one must be a new creature, 1 Thess 4:v16 For the Lord himself shall descend from heaven with a shout. with the voice of the archangel, and with the trump of God; and the dead in christ shall rise first. 2 Cor 5:v17, Therefore if any man be in christ. he is a new creature, old things are passed away, behold,all things are become new.

EPH 4:22-24, That ye put off concerning the former conversation the old man, which is corrupt according to the deceitful lust, v23 And be renewed in the spirit of your mind, v24 And that ye put on the new man, which after God is created in righteousness and true holiness. so be christ at his coming. lcor 15:v23 but every man in his own order, christ the first fruits, afterward they that are christ at his coming.

TO be christ's means that the flesh with all the affections and lusts have been crucified (GAL 5: v24) Rev 20:4-6 And I saw thrones, and they that sat upon them, and judgement was given unto them; and I saw the souls of them that were beheaded for the witness of Jesus and for the word of God, and which had not worshiped the beast, neither his image, neither had received his mark upon their foreheads or in their hands; and they lived and reigned with christ a thousand years, v5,But the rest of the dead lived not again until the thousand years were finished, this is the first resurrection. v6, Blessed and holy is he that hath part in the first resurrection: upon such the second death hath no power, but they shall be priests of God and of christ, and shall reign with him a thousand years.

Heb 12:v14 Follow peace with all men, and holiness, without which no man shall see the Lord. be good" John 5: 28-29 Marvel not at this; for the hour is coming, in the which all that are in the graves shall hear his voice. v29 And shall come forth, they that have done good, unto the resurrection of life; and they that have done evil,unto the resurrection of damnation. Gal 5: 16-24 This I say then, walk in the spirit and ye shall not fulfill the lust of the flesh. v17, For the flesh lusteth against the spirit, and the spirit against the flesh, and these are contrary the one to the other, so that ye cannot do the things that he would. v18, But if be led by the spirit, ye are not under the law. v19, Now the works of the flesh are manifest which are these; Adultery, fornication, uncleanness,lasc iviousness,v20, Idolatry, witchcraft, hatred, variance, emulation, wrath, strife, sedition, heresies, v2l, envying, murders, drunkenness, reveling, and such like of the which I tell you before, as I have also told you in time past that they which do such things shall not inherit the kingdom of God.

v22, But the fruit of the spirit is love, Joy, peace. long suffering, gentleness, goodness, faith, v23, meekness, temperance, against such there is no law. v24, And they that are christ's have crucified the flesh with the affections and lusts. 2 Cor 7:v1, Having therefore these promises, dearly beloved, let us cleanse ourselves from all filthiness of the flesh and spirit, perfecting holiness in the fear of God.

Be in the body of christ. 1 the church which he is coming for (Eph 5: 25-27, Husband love your wives even as christ also love the church, and gave himself for it, v26 That he might sanctify and cleanse it with washing of water by the word. v27, That he present it to himself a glorious church. not having spot, or wrinkle, or any such thing but that it should be holy and without blemish. 1 Cor 13; Eph 1: v22-23, And hath put all things under his feet, and gave him to be the head over all things to the church, v23, Which is his body, the fullness of him that filleth all in all. Col 1:18, And he is the head of the body, the church, who is the beginning, the firstborn from the dead, that in all things he might have the preeminence, v24, Who now rejoice in my sufferings for you, and fill up that which is behind of the afflictions of christ in my flesh for his body's sake which is the church.

Be pure) 1 John 3: 1-3, Behold, what manner of love the father hath bestowed upon us, that we should be called the sons of

God; therefore the world knoweth us not, because it know him not. v2 Beloved" now are we the sons of God, and it" doeth not yet appear what we shall be, but we know that, when he shall appear, we shall be like him, for we shall see him as he is. v3, And every man that hath this hope in him purifieth himself, even as he is pure. Matt 5: v8, Blessed are the pure in heart for they shall see God. Eph 5:v27, That he might present it to himself a glorious church, not having spot, or wrinkle, or any such thing. but that it should be holy and without blemish.

## 1 JOHN 1:7, BE SURE YOU ARE WALKING IN THE LIGHT

*B*ut if ye walk in the light, as he is in the light we have fellowship one with another, and the blood of Jesus christ his son cleanseth us from all sin. CH 2: 6-1l. He that saith he abideth in him aught himself also so to walk, even as he walked. v7, Brethren I write no new commandment unto you. but an old commandment which ye had from the beginning, the old commandment is the word which ye heard from the beginning. v8, Again, a new commandment I write unto you, which thing is true in him and in you, because the darkness is past, and the true light now shineth. v9, He that saith he is in the light, and hateth his brother is in darkness even until now. v10. He that loveth his brother abideth in the light. and there none occasion of stumbling in him. vll, But he that hateth his brother is in darkness, and walketh in darkness, and knoweth not whither he goeth. because that darkness hath blinded his eyes.

CH 3: 9-10 Whosoever is borne of God doeth not commit sin, for his seed remaineth in him; and he cannot sin, because he is born of God. v10, In this the children of God are manifest and the children of the devil; whosoever doeth not righteousness is not of God, neither he that loveth not his brother.

## BE SURE YOU ARE WORTHY

_Luke 21: 34-36, Jesus said) And take heed to yourselves, lest at any time your heart be overcharge with surfeiting, and drunkenness, and cares of this life, and so that day come upon you unawares. v35, For as a snare shall it come on all them that dwell on the face of the whole earth. v36, watch ye therefore, and pray always, that ye may be accounted worthy to escape all these things that shall come to pass, and to stand before the son of man.

This is the plain reference in all scripture to the rapture-of some escaping all the terrible things of v25-28, How were they to escape, if they met the conditions, it is clearly stated how we are to escape and to stand before the son of man (v36) How could all worthy ones go before the son of man if it is not by the rapture as stated in John 14: 1-3, 1 Thess 4:13-18)

Terrible things are coming according to Luke 21: 25-28, Jesus said, And there shall be signs in the sun, and in the moon, and in the stars, and upon the earth distress of nations, with perplexity; the sea and the waves roaring. v26 Men's heart failing them for fear, and for looking after those things which are coming on the earth, for the powers of heaven shall be shaken. v27, And then shall they see the son of man coming in a cloud with power and great glory. v28, And when these things begin to come to pass, then look up and lift up your heads;f or your redemption draweth nigh. One must do all what it takes to escape these things according to the word of God, and to have part in the first resurrection.

The sole purpose of the baptism of the holy spirit is to endue men with power from an high to do the same works that Jesus did. Jesus plainly taught that such an enduement of power was necessary to confirm the word of God, Mark 16:v20. And they went forth, and preaching every where, the Lord working with them, confirming the word with signs following. AMen. Heb 2: 3-4, How shall we escape, if we neglect so great a salvation, which at first began to be spoken by the Lord, and was confirmed unto us by them that heard him. v4 God also bearing them witness, both with signs and wonders, and with divers miracles, and gift of the holy ghost, according to his own will.

Acts 1:v1-2, The former treatise have I made O" the-oph-ilus, of all that Jesus began both to do and teach. v2 Until the day in which he was taken up, after that he began through the holy ghost had given commandment unto the apostles whom he had chosen; Matt 28:v20, Teaching them to observe all things what so ever I have commanded you; and Lo, I am with you always, even unto the end of the world. A-Men.(Acts I:v8) But ye shall receive power, after that the holy ghost is come upon you: and ye shall be witnesses unto me both in Jerusalem, and in all Judaea and in sa-maria, and unto the uttermost part of the earth. and to prove men to be true believers and divinely sent to represent christ.

Mark 16: 15-20, And he said unto them, go ye into all the world, and preach the gospel to every creature. v16, He that be-lieveth and is baptized shall be saved, but he that believeth not shall be damned. v17 And these sign. shall them that believe, in my name shall they cast out devils; they shall speak with new tongues. The source of the believers power is in my name Jesus said, which expresses the power of attorney, if one fully uses this power he will do the works of christ. John 14: 12-15,CH 15: v16,Acts 1:v8,) Mark 16:v18, They shall take up serpents, and if they drink any deadly thing, it shall not hurt them, they shall lay hands on the sick, and they shall recover.

v19, so then after the Lord had spoken unto them, he was received up into heaven, and sat on the right hand of God. v20, And they went forth, and preaching every where, and the Lord working with them, and confirming the word with signs following. A-Men. John 14: v12, verily, verily, I say unto you, he that believeth on me, the works that I do shall he do also, and greater works than these shall he do, because I go unto my father.

# ATTENTION PLEASE

$\mathcal{P}$SALMS 1: and PSALMS 14: is not my idea to put them in the book. After I started to write the book, one night the Lord spoke to me in a vision, I heard these words, have you considered PSALMS 1: and PSALMS 14, 1 did not think of putting them in the book but the Lord have a better idea, the Lord have people that he will be talking to from these PSALMS. for those who do not believe that God talk to people today, I want you to know that this is his portion he put in the book, confirming to me that he sanction my book. The Lord is still working with us when we are doing things for his glory and honour.

PSALM 1: said) Blessed is the man that walketh not in the counsel of the ungodly, nor standeth in the way of sinners, nor sitteth in the seat of the scornful. v2 But his delight is in the law of the Lord, and in his law he doeth meditate day and night. v3, And he shall be like a tree planted by the rivers of water, that bringeth forth his fruit in his season, his leaf also shall not wither, and whatsoever he doeth shall prosper. v4 The ungodly are not so, but are like the chaff which the wind driveth away. v5 Therefore the ungodly shall not stand in the judgment, nor sinners in the congregation of the righteous. v6 For the Lord knoweth the way of the righteous, but the way of the ungodly shall perish.

The emphasis here is on THAT man who live his life to the end of his days the way God created him to live.

PSALM 14: The fool hath said in his heart, there is no God, they are corrupt, they have done abominable works, there is none that doeth good. v2 The Lord looked down from heaven upon the children of men, to see if there were any that did understand, and seek God. v3 They are all gone aside, they are all together become filthy, there is none that doeth good, no, not one. v4 Have all the workers of iniquity no knowledge? who eat up my people as they eat bread, and call not upon the Lord. v5 There were they in great fear, for God is in the generation of the righteous. v6 Ye have shamed the counsel of the poor, because the Lord is his refuge. v7 Oh that the salvation of Israel were come out of zion! when the Lord bringeth back the captivity of his people, Jacob shall rejoice, and Israel shall be glad,

## 12 Characteristics Of Fools

They deny the existence of God:
They live corrupt lives
They do abominable works
They are without understanding
They ignore God-they do not seek him
They are not good, no not one.
They have all gone astray from God
They have become filthy in life
They live in ignorance of God.
They destroy God's people
They never pray
They oppress the poor.

IF Christians found themselves in any of these conditions, they are backsliding and must hurry back to the path of righteousness.

PSALM 15: Lord, who shall abide in thy tabernacle? who shall dwell in thy holy hill? v2 He that walketh uprightly, and worketh righteousness, and speaketh the truth in his heart. v3 He that backbiteth not with his tongue, nor doeth evil to his neighbour, nor taketh up a reproach against his neighbour. v4 IN whose eyes a vile person is contemned; but he honoureth them that fear the Lord, He that sweareth to his own hurt and changeth not. v5 He that putteth not out his money to usury, nor taketh reward against the innocent. He that doeth these things shall never be moved.

The Old testament requirements of salvation in the Bible

are the same as those in the New testament. one must do, and not hear only, as is required in Matt 7: 21-29, on condition of doing the things of v2-5, one will be eternally secure and will never be moved. Matt 7: 21-29, Jesus said) Not every one that saith unto me, Lord, Lord, shall enter into the kingdom of heaven, but he that doeth the will of my father which is in heaven. v22, many will say unto me in that day, Lord, Lord, have we not prophesied in thy name? and in thy name have cast out devils? and in thy name done many wonderful works? v23, And then will I profess unto them, I never knew you, depart from me, ye that work iniquity. v24, Therefore whosoever heareth these sayings of mine, and doeth them, I will liken him unto a wise man, which built his house on a rock;

v25 And the rain descended, and the floods came, and the winds blew, and beat upon that house; and it fell not, for it was founded upon a rock. v26, And every one that heareth these sayings of mine, and doeth them not, shall be liken unto a foolish man, which built his house upon the sand. v27, And the rain descended, and the floods came, and the winds blew, and beat upon that house, and it fell, and great was the fall of it. v28, And it came to pass, when Jesus had ended these sayings, the people were astonished at his doctrine. v29, For he taught them as one having authority; and not as the scribes.

Just as it is true in the natural realm, so it is in the spiritual. A man cannot be a saint and a sinner at the same time. Romans 6:16-23, CH 8:13, This is a death sentence upon professed preachers and Christians who do not bring forth good fruit. john 15: 1-8, no person who merely professing faith in christ and his atoning work will be saved, only those who doeth the will of my father which is in heaven.

Romans 6:16-23, know ye not, that to whom ye yield yourselves servants to obey, his servant ye are to whom ye obey, whether of sin unto death, or of obedience unto righteousness?. v17, But God be thanked that ye were the servants of sin, but ye

✧ ✧ ✧ ✧ ✧ ✧ ✧ ✧ ✧ ✧ ✧ ✧ ✧ ✧ ✧ ✧

have obeyed from the heart that form of doctrine which delivered you. V18, Being then made free from sin, ye become the servants of righteousness. v19, I speak after the manner of men because of the infirmity of your flesh, for as ye have yielded your members servants to uncleanness and to iniquity unto iniquity; even so now yield your members servants to righteousness unto holiness. v20 For when ye were the servants of sin, ye were free from righteousness. v2l, What fruit had ye then in those things whereof ye are now ashamed? for the end of those things is death. v22, But now being made free from sin, and become servants of God, ye have your fruit unto holiness, and the end everlasting life. v23, For the wages of sin is death; but the gift of God is eternal life through Jesus christ our Lord.

There are millions of people today who have not learned these simple-facts-that you cannot be a servant of sin and satan and a servant of righteousness and christ at the same time, that if you commit sin you are a servant of sin and satan. John 8: 34-35, Jesus answered them, verily, verily, I say unto you whosoever committeth sin is the servant of sin. v35, And the servant abideth not in the house for ever, but a son abideth ever.

NO man can commit sin and not be a servant of sin (v34) and no man can sin and not pay the penalty for sin. Gen 2:16-17, And the Lord God commanded the man, saying, of every tree in the garden thou mayest freely eat, v17, But of the tree of the knowledge of good and evil, thou shalt not eat of it; for in the day that thou eatest thereof thou shalt surely die. Ezek 18:v4, Behold, all souls are mine, as the souls of the father, so also the soul of the son is mine; the soul that sinneth, it shall die. Romans 8:12-13, Therefore, brethren, we are debtors, not to the flesh, to live after the flesh. v13, For if ye live after the flesh, ye shall die but if ye through the spirit do mortify the deeds of the body, ye shall live. (to subdue the flesh through self-denial to what the the flesh want to do, put to death the practices of the flesh by the spirit.

1 Cor 6: 9-11, know ye not that the unrighteous shall not

inherit the kingdom of God? be not deceived, neither fornicators, nor idolators, nor adulterers, nor effeminate,(a man who is womanlike) nor abusers of themselves with mankind.

v10, Nor thieves, nor covetous, nor drunkards, nor revilers, nor extortioner, shall inherit the kingdom of God. vll, And such were some of you, but ye are washed, but ye are sanctified, but - ye are justified in the name of the Lord Jesus, and by the spirit of our God. The body is for the Lord, and not for fornication and sin, Christians are not to tolerate any thing that will control them or have authority over them that is not profitable (v13) The thought of this verse is that God has made appetite for food and food for appetite, but he has not made the body for amoral acts, but for the Lord. All sins destroy, but he who commits fornication sins against his entire constitution, even his own body, soul and spirit. v14, And God hath both raised up the Lord, and will also raise us up by his own power.(God has raised Jesus from the dead as a guarantee that he will also raise us up by his own power, so that we may enjoy his eternal blessings and serve him forever.

v15, know ye not that your bodies are the members of Christ? shall I then take the members of Christ, and make them the members of an harlot? God forbid. v16, What? know ye not that he which is joined to an harlot is one body? for two, saith he, shall be one flesh. v17, But he that is joined unto the Lord is one spirit. v18, Flee fornication, every sin that a man doeth is without the body, but he that committeth fornication sinneth against his own body.

### The body must be free from sin as the temple of the Lord

v19, What? know ye not that your body is the temple of the Holy Ghost which is in you, which ye have of God, and ye are not your own. v20,For ye have bought with a price; therefore glorify God in your body, and in your spirit, which are God's. As the slave is the sole property of his master, so are we, having been bought by the precious blood of Christ we are not our own.

## A VISION ABOUT A VERY DIRTY SKIRT WHAT COULD THIS MEAN?

*W*hile I was worshipping at a certain church, one sunday night 2 people was singing and I saw a very dirty skirt in mid air close by where they were standing. The dirty skirt represent somebody's life who are living in sin and need to washed in the blood of the lamb. Rev 7:v14, And I said unto him, Sir,thou knowest, and he said to me, these are they which came out of great tribulation, and have washed their robes, and made them white in the blood of the lamb. For those who refuse to live from sin will not be among those who had their robes white in the blood of the lamb.

## A VISION ABOUT A LADY STANDING IN MID AIR IN THE CHURCH

*T*his is the same church I was worshipping at the time of this vision. ON one sunday morning service was in progress and I saw a lady standing in mid air in the church. The spot where she was standing was very dark but I could not see her face, The interpretation of the vision is according to the scripture this mean that there are people in the church that are walking in darkness and not in the light. 1 John 1:6-7, said, IF we say we have fellowship with him, (that is Jesus) and walk in darkness, we lie, and do not the truth. v7, But if we walk in the light as he is in the light, we have fellowship one with another and the blood of Jesus christ his son cleanseth us from all sin.

This is the chief message christ came to deliver, that God is light and in him there is no darkness at all. Neither Moses nor the prophets ever gave fullness of this message(John 1: v16-17, And his fullness we have received, and grace for grace. v17, For the law was given by Moses, but grace and truth came by Jesus christ. Christ himself is the chief manifestation of God's light to men John 1:1-12, IN the beginning was the word, and the word was with God, and the word was God. v2, The same was in the beginning with God. v3, All things were made by him; and without him was not any thing made that was made. v4, IN him was life, and the life was the light of men. v5, And the light shineth in darkness, and the darkness comprehended it not. v6, There was a man sent from God whose name was John. v7, The same came as a witness, to bear witness of the light, that all men through him might believe. v8, He was not that light, but was sent to bear witness of that light. v9, That was the true light, which lighteth every man that cometh into the world. v10, He was in the world, and the world was made by him, and the world knew him not. vll, He came unto his own, and his own received him not. v12, But as many as received him, to them gave he power to become the sons of God, even to them that believe on his name.

John 3:16-20, For God so loved the world, that he gave his only begotten son, that whosoever believeth in him should not perish, but have everlasting life. v17,For God sent not his son into the world to condemn the world; but that the world through him might be saved. v18, He that believeth on him is not condemn, but he that believeth not is condemned already,because he hath not believed in the name of the only begotten son of God. v19, And this is the condemnation, that light is come into the world, and men loved darkness rather than light, because their deeds were evil.v20,For every one that doeth evil hateth the light, neither cometh to the light, lest his deeds should be reproved.

THE next time the son of God is sent to this world it is to judge matt 16:27, CH 25:31-46, his name means saviour, and any one who does not believe it and take him as such cannot be saved matt 1:21, And she shall bring forth a son, and thou shalt call his name Jesus: for he shall save his people from their sins.

God is a person and dwells in a light that no man can approach unto, whom no man has seen in all his glory nor can see, to whom be honour and power everlasting. AMen.1 Tim 6:v16.) The phrase God is light does not constitute the being of God. It must be understood in the same sense that we understand God is love, God is good, God is a spirit, or God is a consuming fire. And other statements about him, also, in the same sense that Jesus is the way, the truth, and the life. Does these expressions do away with the reality and personality of God and christ, John 4: 24, said) God is a spirit, and they that worship him must worship in spirit and in truth. God is the source of wisdom, knowledge. holiness, God is to man what the sun is to our world, for this reason we can see the importance of the message that God is light and no darkness at all v5).

## THE CHRISTIAN JOY

The Christian joy must be in the Lord and make him your chief joy giver and nothing else. PSALM 100: Make a joyful noise unto the Lord all ye lands. v2, Serve the Lord with gladness, come before his presence with singing. v3, know thee that the Lord he is God.it is he that hath made us, and not we ourselves, we are his people, and the sheep of his pasture. v4, Enter into his gates with thanksgiving, and into his courts with praise, be thankful unto him and bless his name. v5, For the Lord is good, his mercy is everlasting, and his truth endureth to all generations.

PSALM 103: Bless the Lord o my soul, and all that is within me bless is holy name. v2, Bless the Lord o my soul, and forget not all his benefits. v3, Who forgiveth all thine iniquitys, who healeth all thy diseases. v4, Who redeemeth thy life from destruction, who crowneth thee with loving kindness and tender mercies. v5, Who satisfieth thy mouth with good things, so that thy youth is renewed like the eagles.

## THIS WAS HALLELUJAH TIME, DAVID SEEKS TO BRING THE ARK OF THE LORD TO JERUSALEM

$2$ Sam 6: Again, David gathered together all the chosen men of Israel, thirty thousand men. v2, And David rose and went, with all the people that all the people that were with him from

Baal-e of Judah, to bring up from thence the Ark of God,whose name is called by the name of the Lord of hosts that dwelleth between the cherubims.

This was the forth time since David had been anointed king that he gathered the chosen men of Israel, three times to war with all who were gathered, but here he use a limited number.

Instead of the priests carrying the Ark as provided for in the law of Moses 2 Sam 15:24, Exod 37:v5, NUM 4:15. A new cart was made to bring the Ark to Jerusalem. This was also the way the philistines send it back to Israel. 1-SAM 6:v7.

2 SAM 6:14, And David danced before the Lord with all his might, and David was girded with a linen ephod. v15, SO David and all the house of Israel brought up the Ark of the Lord with shouting, and with the sound of the trumpet. v16, And as the Ark of the Lord came into the city of David, Mi-chal Saul's daughter looked through a window, and saw king David leaping and dancing before the Lord, and she despised him in her heart.

This was the garment for priests and levites and not for kings, but since he was a type of christ who was to be priest-king (Zech 6:12-13) David was allowed by God to use it on this occasion, or else such was overlooked by him like the show bread that he ate when he was fleeing from Saul, 1 SAM 21:3-6. Jesus reffered to this in showing that rituals was made for man, and not man for rituals and therefore, man was lord of such, even if it seemed unlawful(Matt 12: 3-5, Mark 2: 23-28)

Apparently David put off his royal robes and dressed in the robe of a servant of God as an act of homage, tribute. respect, reverence, to God who dwelled between the cherubim on the Ark

✧ ✧ ✧ ✧ ✧ ✧ ✧ ✧ ✧ ✧ ✧ ✧ ✧ ✧ ✧ ✧ ✧

which was transferring to its place in the new capital of Israel. David was critised by his wife Mi-chal, she and David were not the same where the joy of the Lord was concern. her words were bitter, she did not let David feel welcome, but rather despised him in her heart. she was proudish because she did not know what it mean to rejoice and praise God, and the Lord punish her for it, he made her childless unto her death(v22-23)

It is sad to say that there are churches like that today, they do not have what it takes to rejoice and praise God. they are only a shell of what the church of God suppose to be. It appears these people do not have anything to rejoice and praise God for but David did. v2l, David said unto Mi-chal his wife, it was before the Lord, which chose me before thy father. and before all his house, to appoint me ruler over the people of the Lord, over Israel, therefore I will play before the Lord. David greatly appreciate how the Lord took him from a shepherd field and anointed him and made him king over his people Israel, so he dance, and he dance, and he dance.

IF you rejoice, and shout in some church today they will despise you and even put you out, they claim we are disturbing their service, and they could be right, that mean the church is theirs and not the Lord's because in God's church people rejoice and praise him who hath called us out of darkness into his marvelous light. Any church that resist against the working of the spirit of God cannot blessed spiritually, because the Lord resist the proud and giveth grace to the humble, they will always be cold, lukewarm, dry, empty, and dead. The holy spirit is the one that giveth life to the church without him church dead. Rejoicing and dancing and praising God is not a new testament doctrine, God's people was rejoicing and praising him long before Jesus was born. If the church is the Lord's he have the right to do what he will in his own church and with his own people.

God's church is not a quiet and cold church, It is a church where God's people rejoice and shout hallelujah making joyful noise unto the Lord. Neh 8:v10, the joy of the Lord is our strength, so be joyful and bless his name. For God's People to retain the joy of the Lord means that we must abide in his love. John 15:v6, Jesus said) IF a man abide not in me, he is cast forth as a branch and is withered, and men gather them, and cast them into the fire, and they are burned. v10, IF ye keep my commandment, ye shall abide in my love, even as I have kept my father's commandment, and abide in his love. vll, These things have I spoken unto you, that my joy might remain in you, and that your joy might be full.

The secret to the Christian joy and have our prayer answered is to live in obedience to the word of God. For a Christian to live sinful lives mean that you will lose your joy, you will be cut off like the branch of a tree and withered and die. Christians are under obligation to obey the gospel throughout life and not only when we are at church.

### WHY CHRISTIANS REJOICE AND PRAISE GOD?

*I*N PSALM 34: David said) I will bless the Lord at all times: his praise shall continually be in my mouth. v2, My soul shall make her boast in the Lord: the humble shall hear thereof, and be glad. v3,0 magnify the Lord with me, and let us exalt his name together. we must respect, reverence,honor God, and have no fear of man. God did not save you to live in fear of man, you must be free to rejoice and praise God where ever you go.

We rejoice and praise God because of what Jesus did on the cross of calvary for us in order to redeem our soul, many of us were great sinners, we were no body.

'But now, 1 Peter 2: 9-10, But now ye are a chosen generation, a royal priesthood, an holy nation, a peculiar people, that ye should shew forth the praises of him who hath called you out of darkness into his marvellous light. v10, Which in time past were not a people, but are now the people of God, which had not obtained mercy, but now have obtained mercy. The people of God must be bold strong and vibrant. Jesus said, Ye are the salt of the earth: but if the salt lost his savour, taste, flavor, wherewith shall it be salted? it is thenceforth good for nothing, but to cast out, and to be trodden under foot of men matt 5:13). And these things write we unto you, that your joy may be full. 1 John 1:v4).

I cannot see a cold, dry, dead church that have no joy showing forth the praises of him who hath called us out of darkness into his marvellous light. IF such is the case, ask the Lord to fill you with the holy ghost and fire, and your joy will be full. IN the last day, that great day of the feast, Jesus stood and cried, saying, if any man thirst,let him come unto me, and drink. He that believeth on me, as the scripture hath said, out of his belly shall flow rivers of living water. john 7:37-38).

Jesus compare the baptism of the holy spirit as a river, a river is not a stagnant body of water, a river flows, we can see it, we can hear it, so likewise is the holy spirit, we can see the manifestation of the holy spirit upon the believer, we can see the anointing on the believer, we can feel him, he is very much alive in us filling our hearts with joy, real joy.

## A VISION OF ENCOURAGEMENT

The Lord gave me a few words of encouragement in a night vision in the year 2005, for the people who do not dream dreams or see visions do not know the effect that these revelation carries. I heard the voice of the Lord said unto me, press along saint press along. To me I think the Lord is saying keep running son the race is almost won. He is cheering me on, how nice this is marvellous. When a child of God hear words like these from the Lord himself, they mean much, they inspire the believer, they are words of encouragement. so I am passing these few words of encouragement unto you, that in the midst of your trials, and temptation, at a time when you feel like no one cares, remember Jesus cares, so press along saint press along the battle is almost won. Brothers and sisters in the Lord, you may not hear the voice of the Lord like I have but he is cheering you on just the same, his heart desire is for you to overcome as he have overcome, you may have tears in your eyes but remember weeping may endure for a night, but joy cometh in the morning. PSALMS 30:v5).

## ATTENTION PLEASE, DO YOU BELIEVE THAT THE HOLY SPIRIT HAS A VOICE AND THAT HE DO SPEAK?

*Y*ou may be very surprise to hear this, but it is true. I would like to sharpen your consciousness about the holy spirit that we have living inside of us. The Lord gave me many experiences but I do not believe that the Lord gave them to me to be thrown into the trash basket and no body know about them. IN 1 Cor 6: 19-20, Paul ask, What? know ye not that your body is the temple of the Holy Ghost which is in you, which ye have of God, and ye are not your own. v20,For ye are bought with a price, therefore glorify God in your body, and in your spirit which are God's.

It was in the year 2006, that night I prayed and went to bed, and I heard the voice of the Holy Spirit greet me, he said, hi brother grey, I was not sleeping, it was just a few minutes after I went to bed, I am 100 percent sure that I was not sleeping, the Lord is my witness I lie not. The voice spoke to me from inside of me, I am 100 percent sure of that. the voice of the Holy Spirit is very fine, much, much, finer than any human voice, but distinctly clear. I know there are people that will have problems believing these things, they will say it did not happen, they will argue as if they know what God will say from that which he will not say, or who he would talk to, you don't know that, none of us know that. so please don't sin yourself over this matter, unless you want the devil to use you to stop other people from believing.

We humans know how to entertain our friends and love ones, we try to make them comfortable, but how are we treating this important heavenly guest, (the holy spirit) is he happy, is he comfortable in the house where he live, or he is very unhappy because of the way you live. The Holy spirit is a person and must be treated with respect and honour, the HOLY Spirit can be grieved, Paul write in Eph 4:v3O, And grieve not the Holy spirit of God, where by ye are sealed unto the day of redemption.

The Holy spirit is the one who is giving us the power to do the work of christ, our joy, and peace, and anointing come from him, if he should walk away because of the way he was treated, we would lukewarm, cold, dry, and spiritually dead. It is very important that you are on good terms with your heavenly guest (the Holy Spirit). SO let us worship the Lord our God in spirit and in truth, and not as hypocrites.

## ALL SPIRITUAL OPPOSITION IS SATANIC

Since God is the author of all scripture then God does not become an opposition against himself, then all spiritual gifts 'and blessings in the church today is of God. Any one who criticize spiritual experiences is of the devil, because the devil is the author of all criticism. Some people have no respect for the gifts and blessings that God give to other Christians, they rather criticize you to humiliate you and shut you up, this is satanic. The Bible said we are to rejoice with them that rejoice, and weep with them that weep. When some one criticize and condemn these experiences when it is clearly stated in scripture, it is a tool of the devil to rob God's people of the purpose and benefits of these experience.

## CHRISTIANS SHOULD UNITE TO FIGHT THE DEVIL

The time Christians waste criticizing and fighting one another, we should unite to fight sin, sickness, and the devil, knowing that we have a common foe (satan). AS long as the devil can get Christians to fight each other he know they will not be united to fight him. THE devil agitate men to differ over church creeds, rituals, and petty theories in doctrines, and even to condemn each other over spiritual experiences that there should be no difference. The devil plan is to keep men from getting power with God over him and his works. The devil let men create all kind of doctrines and false doctrines to create disunity so that we are not unite to fight against him. AS long as he can keep Christians from making war against him and from getting power with God to defeat him he will be free to continue his work of sin to defeat and destroy the lives of men and women.

## WHAT IS THE GOAL OF EVERY CHRISTIAN?

The goal of every Christian should be to achieve all the fullness of God until the full evidences of the baptism of the Holy Ghost are manifested in their lives. No one should be satisfied with just a measure of the spirit that they now has, but it is sad to say that the least blessings from the Lord seems to satisfied the average person.

## NO ONE SHOULD CRITICIZE THE EXPERIENCES OF OTHERS

Many of us have heard slanderous remarks about people who claim divine healing power, who claim to have been healed by the power of God, who claim the baptism of the Holy Spirit, or some one who claim some other biblical experience. Some people chose to ridiculed all manifestation of the supernatural while hundreds of thousands of people in our biggest churches know nothing of real truth along these lines. Church members are taught to shun any mention of these biblical doctrines and to class all spiritual manifestation to be of the devil or as fanaticism. All spiritual gift in the church is of God.

## ALL SPIRITUAL MANIFESTATION ARE STRANGE

*T*he apostle Paul said that the things of the spirit of God are foolishness to the natural man 1 Cor 2: v14, and that God would take the foolish things of the world to confound the wise (lcor 1: 26-31) naturally any manifestation of any one of the nine gifts of the spirit recorded in 1 Cor 12: would be foolishness and very strange to any man who had never seen them-.,in operation. But why reject or criticize something that you know nothing about either scripturally experimentally? The natural man is not use to any spiritual experience and every one of them will be foolishness to him until he make up his mind to be open enough to them to investigate the truth from what is written about them.

When something is clearly written about from the word of God concerning spiritual blessings that should settle the matter as being biblical and to be the word of God. Then this should help the natural man to understand and accept the truth.

Paul said that there are diversities of operations, but the same God which worketh all in all. and that there are diversities of gifts, gifts, but the same spirit, and that the manifestation of the spirit is given to every man to profit withal. How can any one criticize when they do not know what manifestation will come. 1 Cor 12:

## A VISION ABOUT A BEAUTIFUL GARDEN AND A CHURCH

*I*t was in the year 2006, that the Lord gave me this vision. One night I dream seeing a beautiful garden and a church, the fruits and vegetables was green and fat, I could see that the garden was 100 percent cared for. While I was at that church I was on two days of fasting and prayer, I was asking the Lord to raise up people to praise his great name, to give us a revival and change the condition of the church, then the Lord gave me this dream. Where the garden was that area was a part of the congregation at one point, but no one was sitting there any more, so they set up the garden in that area, so the garden and the church is one. That beautiful garden represent the church, it is an illustration or picture of how the Lord want the church to be.

Where the congregation was seated, there was a white man in front the congregation jumping and shouting and praising God, he was very, very, happy and a white lady that was sitting in front of the congregation shouted at him and ask, why are you doing that? because she never see any one did that in the church before, and the man answered and said, this is the way it should be, this is the way it should be. It is clear from this vision that the Lord do not enjoy a quiet church, he want his people to rejoice and praise him because he is worthy of our praise a billion times over, if we have had ten thousand tongue we would never be able to praise him enough, So let us praise him for what he had done for us.

## THE CHURCH AND THE GARDEN

The dream is one, the garden is the church, the Lord want the church to be just like that beautiful garden. But it sad to say that there are many churches today that are no where close to what God want them to be. They are just like the garden in Isaiah 5: which speak about the Jewish people.

(8) FOLD DESCRIPTION OF GOD'S VINEYARD
1 Jehovah has a vineyard in a very fruitful hill,
2 He fenced it,
3 He gather out all the stones from it,
4 He planted it with the choicest vine,
5 HE BUILt a tower in the midst of it,
6 He made a winepress in it,
7 He expected it to bring forth good grapes,
8 It brought forth wild grapes.

✧  ✧  ✧  ✧  ✧  ✧  ✧  ✧  ✧  ✧  ✧  ✧  ✧  ✧  ✧

(3) THINGS GOD ASK JUDAH TO DO

1 TO judge between him and his vineyard and decide certain matters.
2 Tell Jehovah what he should have done that he had not done to make his vineyard produce good grapes.
3 Tell him why it brought forth wild grapes when he had planted the choicest vine.

The Lord was very disappointed because he had done all that was to be done to his vineyard and it did not produce good grapes, so he pronounce judgement upon his vineyard.

1 I will take away the hedge from it,
2 the vineyard shall be eaten up,
3 I will break down the wall from around it,
4 the vineyard shall be trodden down,
5 I will lay it waste
6 I will not prune or cultivate it
7 there shall come up briers and thorns
8 I will command the clouds that no rain will fall on it.

## THE CHRISTIAN CHURCH

1 Tell the Lord what he should have done that he have not done
2 Jesus gave his life on a cruel cross for you and I
3 He redeem your soul
4 He put your name in the lambs book of life
5 He deliver you out of a horrible pit
6 He gave you his holy spirit
7 He send his holy angels to watch over you
8 He put a song in your heart and make you glad
9 He made us sons and daughters

10 He made us a people when we were not a people

11 He made us a chosen generation

12 He made us a royal priesthood

13 He made us a holy nation and a peculiar people

14 He forgive our sins and made us righteous through the blood of Jesus christ the son of God.

After all these wonderful blessings the Lord has given to us and blessed us with, he look forward to see us produce fruits of righteousness, but with many Christians the Lord is very disappointed, because they only produce bad fruits. They refuse to live holy. The reason why many Christians cannot bear good fruit is because they are not abiding in christ. IN John 15: 4-6, Jesus said, Abide in me, and I in you, as the branch cannot bear fruit of itself, except it abide in the vine, no more can ye, except ye abide in me. v5, I am the vine, ye are the branches; He that abideth in me, and I in him the same bringeth forth much fruit, for without me ye can do nothing. v6, IF a man abide not in me, he is cast forth as a branch and is withered, and men gather them, and cast them into the fire, and they are burned. Except believers abide in christ we are powerless. But it is sad to say that many Christians are given up to their reprobate mind, to-do what ever they choose, it mean they are depraved, cast off by God, disapprove of rejected. This is what happen to Christian who will not give up sin.

Romans 1: 21-32, Because that, when they knew God, they glorified him not as God, neither were they thankful, but became vain in their imaginations, and their foolish heart was darkened. v22, professing themselves to be wise, they became fools. v24, wherefore God also gave them up to uncleanness through the lust of their own hearts, to dishonor-,-their own bodies between themselves. v26, For this cause God gave them up unto vile affections, for even their women did change the natural use into that which is against nature. v27 And likewise also the men, leaving the natural use of the woman, burned in their lust one toward another, men with men working that which is unseemly, and receiving in themselves that recompence of their error which was meet. v28, And even as they did not like to retain God in their knowledge; God gave them over to a reprobate mind, to do those things which are not convenient. v29, Being filled with all unrighteousness, fornication, wickedness, covetousness, maliciousness, full of envy, murder, debate, deceit, malignity, people who speak evil of other people, they cause strife, whispers.

## SINS THAT WILL DAMN THE SOUL

$\mathcal{G}$al 5: 19-2l, Paul said, Now the works of the flesh are manifested, which are these. Adultery, fornication, uncleanness, Lasciviousness. v20, Idolatry, witchcraft, hatred, variance, emulations, warth strife, sedition, Heresies. v2l, envying, murders, drunkenness, revelings, and such like, of the which I tell you before, as i have also told you in time past,that they which do such things shall not inherit the kingdom of God.

## A VISION OF PROPHECY CONCERNING RUSSIA, (FULFILLED

$\mathcal{T}$his is a very important prophecy in our days, l want the world to know that the God of Israel and the prophets still ruleth in the kingdom men. It was in the year 1972 when the Lord gave me this prophecy. One night the Lord spoke me in a night vision and said, in 1989 will be the judgement of Antichrist, I prophesy in the church to the hearing of every one, and said thus saith the Lord in 1989 will be the judgement of antichrist. I waited 17 years for this prophecy to be fulfilled, in 1989 right on target RUSSIA fell, just as the Lord had said. The gift of prophecy is alive and well. The fall of RUSSIA send a shock wave across the world, many questions was ask, about what happen to RUSSIA, other communist countries fell along with them.

RUSSIA must fall because she had countries under her control that belong to the old Roman Empire, like Bulgaria, Romania, Hungary, and Albania. RUSSIA would never give up any of these territory without war and for that reason the God of heaven and earth take away the power of RUSSIA so that the countries under her control would be free to be a member of the European Union, proving once again that the God of heaven ruleth in the kingdom of men Daniel 4: 17, Nebuchadnezzar king of Babylon learn this lesson the hard way.

## THE OLD ROMAN EMPIRE WILL RISE AGAIN, SETTING THE STAGE FOR THE MAN OF SIN, THE ANTICHRIST

*A*nd the forth kingdom shall be as strong as iron, in as much as iron break in pieces and subdueth all things; and as iron that breaketh all these, so shall the forth kingdom break in pieces and crush all the others"(Daniel 2:40). After the prophet Daniel given the interpretation of king Nebuchadnezzar's dream, he later had a vision of his own. After this I saw in a night vision and behold, a fourth beast, dreadful and terrible, exceedingly strong, and break in pieces, and stamping the residue with the feet of it, and it was different from all the beast that were before it; and it had ten horns Daniel 7:v7).

## THE REVIVAL OF THE OLD ROMAN EMPIRE

*T*he two visions in Daniel chapter 2: about the great metallic image and the four great wild beast in Daniel 7; are different prophetic view of the same successive series of four world Empires that would rule the world until the coming of Jesus christ as the Messiah.

Ancient Rome, the fourth world Empire, began as an insignificant city state but quickly rose to power, over all of Italy in the third century before christ. IN its ongoing rivalry in north Africa, the Romans conquered most of northern Africa and the Greek Empire during the second century before christ. Nations fell one after the other before the well disciplined and brutal legions of the

Romans, the caesars finally ruled virtually the whole of the known world by the time of christ.

The fourth beast is a symbol of the old Roman Empire. The fourth of four kingdom in succession. It is mentioned by name only in the N.T. Paul called him, the man of sin, and son of perdition 2 Thess 2:v3. This is a non discript beast for there is nothing on earth to compare it with.

It is a dreadful terrible, strong beast with great iron teeth symbolizing the same as the iron on the image of Daniel 2:40-43 in fulfillment it devoured the other beasts and stamped upon them with its feet, which mean it conquered all the territories of the first beasts-Babylon, medo-persia, and Greece. It was different from all the beasts before it, not only in a republican form of government, but also in power, greatness, extent of dominion and length of duration. The ten horns symbolize ten kingdoms in the latter days, the last form of the old Roman Empire v7-8, 23-24, Rev 13: CH 17: 8-17). Horns always symbolize kings. The horns were the last parts of the beast seen by Daniel, and are therefore considered last here v8)23-24, Rev 17: 12-17).

## THE LITTLE HORN

The little horn came up last after the ten horns were fully grown. It plucked up three of the ten by the roots symbolizing the the Antichrist, coming in the last days of the formation of

Rome into 10 kingdoms. He will overthrow 3 of them and the others will submit to him without further war (v8, 23-24, Rev 17:11-17 The little horn is a man who speaks blasphemies against God v8, 25; Rev ll:v36, Rev 13:1,5, CH 17:v3,) From the time of Babylon until the judgment of v9-10, the Antichrist will be defeated at the second coming of christ vll-14.

Thrones and judgment were set or placed. This refers to the judgment of the nations v26, Matt 25: 31-46). This is God the father, not christ who is seen as a separate person from Ancient of days in v13-14. Both are seen as separate persons by the same prophet and at the same place, so there must be at least 2 persons in the Godhead, The fact is, there are three of them, father, son, and Holy spirit.

## LIST OF EUROPEAN UNION MEMBER STATES BY ACCESSION.

$\mathscr{T}$his is a list of European union member states, their dates of application and accession. It shows the growth of the European union and its predecessors through enlargement from six members in 1952 to twenty five in 2004 and twenty-seven members in 2007, as of 2006, at least seven (possible even more) are expected to join in its future.

The European union per se was created on november 1/1993 when the treaty on European union came into effect. Twelve of the current 25 member states joined one of the union predecessors, either the European coal and steel community (which came into existence on July 23/1952 and ceased to exist exactly 50 years later), the European Economic community(which came into existence on January 1/1958) or the European community (which came into existence on July 1/1967 as a merger of ECSC, EEC and the European Atomic Energy community, and is one of three pillars of the European union today.

## CANDIDATE COUNTRIES

$\mathscr{S}$ee also; Enlargement of the European union, Bulgaria and the European union, Croatia and the European union, Republic of Macedonia and the European union, Romania and the European union, and Turkey and the European union.

IN addition to the current 25 member states, a number of other European states will join the European union in the next two decades. Bulgaria and Romania have already finish accession negotiations and will join on January 1/2007. The ratification pro-

✧ ✧ ✧ ✧ ✧ ✧ ✧ ✧ ✧ ✧ ✧ ✧ ✧ ✧ ✧ ✧

cess of the treaty of Accession 2005, which forms the legal framework for the accession of Bulgaria and Romania, was completed on 2006-11-24 when the German Bundesrat voted in favour.

Croatia, the Republic of macedonia and Turkey are officially candidate countries; Croatia and Turkey are currently in accession negotiations while negotiations with the Republic of Macedonia are expected to start in 2007. The remaining states in the Balkans (Albania, Bosnia and Herzegovina, MONTENEGRO and Serbia, including Kosovo under united Nations Security Council Resolution 1244 of June 10/1999) are officially" potential candidate countries", which means they have a clear perspective for accession over the course of the next decade.

The European union's Enlargement Commissioner Olli Rehn originally stated that the next enlargement after Bulgaria and Romania would only happen after 2010, due to the European union's need to sort out its institutional problems first, the European Commission's president Jose Manuel Durao Barroso later stated that the provisions in the Treaty of Nice were clear enough; while he considered institutional reform necessary, it was not intended to be a stumbling bloc for countries to seek to join the European union. However, on 25 September 2006 (the day before the accession date of Bulgaria and Romania was officially made public). Barroso stated that a new treaty would be necessary before further enlargement could occur.

## FUTURE PROSPECTS

*S*ee also; Armenia and the European union, Cape verde and the European union, Georgia and the European union, Iceland and the European union, Israel and the European union, Moldova and the European union, and Ukraine and the European union. It is generally assumed that even with the accession of the states of Southeastern Europe, the process of enlargement will not be finished.

## EUROPEAN COUNTRIES

$\mathscr{A}$rmenia, GEORGIA, Moldova, and Ukraine have stated they would like to join the European union; However, the European union's response was lukewarm at best. European union membership is also the subject of political debate in Andorra, Azerbaijan, the Faroe Islands, Iceland, liechtenstein and San Marino, and the debates in Norway and Switzerland are also still ongoing. While Belarus and Russia are also seen as eligible to join, and while accession to the European union enjoys public support in Belarus, the lack of democratic structures make these countries' impossible in the short term, especially as the European union is supporting the Belarussian opposition and civil society in peacefully overthrowing Alexander Lukashenko's regime, which it regards as dictatorial, going so far as to offer concrete benefits for democratic reforms. Furthermore, the European Union is trying to bind Russia more strongly to its own policies and goals through partnership and cooperation agreements.

## NON-EUROPEAN COUNTRIES

$\mathscr{A}$lthough the treaty of Maastricht states that only European countries may apply, a number of countries not generally considered European have also considered membership bids.

The island nation of Cape Verde, part of the island region Macaronesia (which is comprised of Cape Verde, the portuguese islands of the Azores and Madeira and the Spanish Canary Islands) has stated it wishes to join the European Union. Israel has considered applying for membership; while the European Union and Israel share a common culture, history and society, the on-going Arab-Israeli and Israeli-palestinian conflicts and Israel's location in one of the most conflict-ridden regions of the world would be major arguments against its accession. Finally, even Canada's accession has occasionally been proposed, though often rather in a tongue-in-cheek, manner, the main arguments used are very similar cultural standards and viewpoints on matters of international laws, especially when juxtaposed with those of the United States. None of the three countries is a member of the council of Europe, which a de facto prerequisite for membership under the Copenhagen criteria and the Treaty of Maastricht.

It is generally expected that the states of southeastern Europe will be the next states to join the European Union, and that it will still take some time for Iceland, Norway and Switzerland to join, since public opinion is not yet in favour in those three states. Although Olli Rehn said on May 19/2006 that he expected Iceland to join the European Union before Croatia would; he went back on his statement when he stated on December 1/2006 that CROATIA would likely become the European Union's 28th member state.

## THE BEAST OUT OF THE SEA AND THE EARTH REV 13:1-18

*R*ev 13: is a prophecy of two men who will fulfill what is predicted here during the last three and one-half years of the age.

## THE BEAST OUT OF THE SEA (REV 13:1-10,18)

*F*irst let us examine this passage to see what it has to say about the beast out of the sea. This is a symbol and must be treated as such. The sea is symbolic of peoples (Daniel 7:2,3; Rev 17:1,15,). THE beast in Revelation reveals to the rise of a kingdom, and more particularly to the Antichrist, the earthly head of the kingdom (Rev 13: 18). It also symbolizes a supernatural spirit out of the bottomless pit as we shall see later. Beast in scripture symbolize kingdoms and kings (Dan 2: 37-39; CH 7:2-7 with CH 7:17,23), as well as supernatural powers which control the kingdoms. The personal Antichrist, his power, source of power, worship, characteristics, mouth, titles, wars, exaltation, reign, length of reign, etc, are subject of this passage. They are briefly dealt with as follows;

◇ ◇ ◇ ◇ ◇ ◇ ◇ ◇ ◇ ◇ ◇ ◇ ◇ ◇ ◇ ◇ ◇ ◇ ◇ ◇

Who is the Antichrist? at the present time this question cannot be answered. This question can only be answered when the Antichrist personally make the seven years covenant with Israel (Dan 9: 27) many have speculating that the pope, stalin, a magician or others will be the Antichrist. THEY speculated that Hitler, Mussolini, or other in the past would become the Antichrist but they all failed to be the Antichrist. They turned their faces against the inspiration of prophecy and because of this they speak rubbish.

The Antichrist) where will he come from? This question is fully answered by studying the book of Daniel. After the formation of the ten kingdoms Dan7:7-8,19-25, the revised Roman Empire, the Antichrist will come from among them, he is called the little horn. This mean Russia and communism will be defeated, Russia must give up her control of Austria, Hungary, Romania, Bulgaria, Albania, and all parts of the old Roman Empire. This I can say with all authority that Russia and communism will never rule the world. It is just natural that you would like to know when will the Antichrist revealed himself as Antichrist in world affairs? This question is also clearly answered in scripture; IN Dan 7: 24, we have definite proof that the Antichrist cannot be revealed and be prominent in world affairs, until after the ten kingdoms are formed inside the old Roman Empire according to this verse, the ten kingdoms must be formed and exist for some time as the revised Roman Empire.

The Antichrist will rise and gain the whole ten kingdoms in the first three and one half years of the week. By the middle of the week he will be seen as the beast of Rev 13: coming up out of the sea of humanity already with seven heads and ten horns, which he will have conquered before the middle of the week. His coming out of the sea in the middle of the week will be simple the recognition of his power by the ten kings and the dragon (Rev 13:2-4, CH 17:12-17). This verse further teaches, that because of his rise out of the ten kingdoms, he is to come out of obscurity and that his rise to power will be quick. Daniel saw the little horn, symbolizing an llth king who will come out of one of the ten kingdoms and use it to overthrow 3 others (Dan 7: 7-8,20,23-24, CH 8: 20-25, CH-11:35-45). The other six of the ten will then submit to him, the Antichrist, without further war.

God at this time will put it into the hearts of all the ten to agree and give their power to the beast to fulfill prophecy Rev 17: 8-17. Therefore, no man can tell who the Antichrist will be until after the ten kingdoms are formed.

The Antichrist cannot be revealed until after the rapture as proved in 2 Thess 2: 6-8 And now ye know what with holdeth that he might be revealed in his time. v7 For the mystery of iniquity doth already work; only he who now letteth will let, until he be taken out of the way. v8 And then shall that wicked be revealed, whom the Lord shall consume with the spirit of his mouth, and shall destroy with the brightness of his coming.

Question, What was it that they knew hindered the mystery of iniquity or spirit of lawlessness? if they knew what it was can we not know the same thing, especially in view of this added revelation about it.

When he who hinders is taken out of the way, then shall the wicked be revealed (v7-8). Antichrist cannot possible come to power until after the rapture of the church 1 Thess 4: 13-16, All those who go in the rapture will not be here during during the days of the Antichrist and the tribulation period Rev 6:1-19, 21, and Matt 24: 15-21, Dan 12:v1, I am 100 percent sure that there will be a rapture because I have seen it for myself some years ago, and I also know that on the day of the rapture Jesus will not come to the earth because I saw him standing in mid air and the saints went up to meet him. This is my own true experience with the Lord.

How long will he reign? Antichrist will reign over one of the ten kingdoms of the revised Roman Empire at the beginning of the week and will get power over all ten kingdoms during the last three and one half years (Rev 13:v5, CH 7: 25, CH 12:7). It will be in these last three and one half years that Antichrist will exalt himself above every God and will be worshiped by many of his subjects (Rev 13:14-18; Dan 8:25, CH 11: 36-45, 2 Thess 2: 4). During part of the last three and one-half years Antichrist will reign in Jerusalem" in the glorious.-holy mountain" where the temple will be rebuilt (Dan 11: 45). He will sit in the temple of God, showing himself that he is God.)(2 Thess 2:v4 The temple is where the abomination and desolation will take place Dan 9:27, CH 12:7-13;-Matt 24: 15-22, Rev 11:1,2; CH 13: 12-18).

Babylon will be the place the Antichrist will reign and not Rome. The fact is that there will be ten separate kingdoms with separate capitals and ten separate kings in the first three and one-half years shows that up to the middle of the week the Antichrist does not have one capital where he reigns over the ten kingdoms, for they will not yet under him. Rome will be just one of the ten capitals and her king will reign over the territory of Italy and her possessions and not over all of Revised Rome. It is only when Antichrist become head of all ten kingdoms by the middle of the week that he will establish one control throne in Jerusalem for all the newly formed Empire. Even then, the kings will continue as kings under him(Rev 17:9-17).

Where will the power of Antichrist come from

The power of Antichrist will come from satan, this is an evil spirit out of the Abyss or the bottomless pit, and the ten kings. His power has already been predicted by GOD and it will be given to him in due time.

It is God who will permit satan and his demon agents to give there power to them and inspire them in his evil work.(Dan 8: v24, And his power shall be mighty, but not by his own power, and he shall destroy wonderfully, and shall prosper, and practice, and shall destroy the mighty and holy people. 2 Thess 2:8-12, And then shall that wicked be revealed, whom the Lord shall consume with the spirit of his mouth, and shall destroy with the brightness of his coming. v9 Even him, whose coming is after the working of

❖ ❖ ❖ ❖ ❖ ❖ ❖ ❖ ❖ ❖ ❖ ❖ ❖ ❖ ❖ ❖ ❖

satan with all power and signs and lying wonders, v10, And with all deceivableness of unrighteousness in them that perish; because they received not the love of the truth, that they might be saved.

Why is God permitting apostasy and strong delusion

vll And for this cause" God shall send them strong delusion, that they should believe a lie. v12 That they all might be damned who believe not the truth, but had pleasure in unrighteousness. Also Rev 13: 1,2. It is God who will put it into the hearts of the ten kings to give him their power for the purpose of destroying Mystical Babylon (Rev 17: 12-17) It is the satanic prince out of the Abyss or bottomless pit (Rev 11: 7, CH 17: v8) who will be the executive of satan's power to the beast and who will inspire and back the Antichrist in all his diabolical activities.

Satan will give to Antichrist the kingdoms of the world that he offered Jesus. Again, the devil taketh him up into an exceeding high mountain, and sheweth him all the kingdom of the world, and the glory of them; And saith unto him, all these things will I give thee, if thou wilt fall down and worship me. Then saith Jesus unto him, Get thee hence Satan: for it is written, Thou shalt worship the Lord thy God, and him only shalt thou serve. Matt 4: 8-10). The Antichrist will accept them, Jesus did not,, Antichrist w-ill ' have to fight to possess them even as christ would have had to do and will yet have to do. Antichrist will succeed in this world conquest by conquering the Revised Roman Empire by the middle of week and all the northern and eastern countries of Asia and Europe by the end of the week. Also he will get the co-operation of many other nations, through the ministry of the three unclean spirits who will help him against the Jews and christ at the second advent. After his defeat at Armageddon by christ, Antichrist will be cast into the lake of fire. The kingdom of God will succeed his kingdom and extend throughout the, earth.

## THE VISION OF DANIEL (DAN 7: 1-12

*I*N this section of Daniel we have the prophetical visions of Daniel concerning world events from his day to the second coming of christ and the eternal kingdom of the God of heaven. These visions are all interpreted by God to the prophet and are plainly recorded so there can be no misunderstanding as to any detail. The prophet did not give us his own opinion concerning these visions it was the Lord who gave him the interpretations. The visions are as follows.

## THE VISION OF THE FOUR BEAST(DAN 7: 1-27)

*I*N Dan 2: God shows the Gentile world kingdoms to Nebuchadnezzar from the human standpoint, as a great and beautiful metallic image. IN Dan 7: God shows the prophet Daniel the same kingdoms from the standpoint of ferocious wild beast. The beast are symbols of kingdoms as clearly seen in DAN 7:v17, These four great beast, are four kings, which shall arise out of the earth. All scriptural language is to be taken literally where it is at all possible, or unless there are some clearly stated reason that the language is not to be taken literally.

Even all the figurative language is to be interpreted by that which is literal. That the language in the visions of DAN 7: and 8 are symbolic is clear from the fact that both of these chapters are interpreted for us in detail by an Angel from heaven. SO man's interpretation is no more necessary than it is in understanding DAN 2: concerning the metals of the image. The only thing anyone have to do is to accept God's own interpretation and every symbol in these chapters will be clear.

Winds in symbolic passages denote wars, strife, and judgments from God Jer 25:32-33, Rev 7: 1-3, with CH 8: 7-13, Dan 7:1-3). Seas represent peoples (Rev 17:15). Beasts represent kingdoms and rulers (Dan 7:17,23-24, CH8: 20-23; Rev 13:1-18, CH 17:8-17) Heads represent kingdoms (Dan 7:6; CH 8:20-23, Rev 17: 8-17,) and horns represent kings or rulers of kingdoms (Dan7: 23-24, Rev 17:12-17) The vision itself is recorded in Dan 7: 1-14, and the interpretation is given in Dan 7: 15-28.

## THE LION, DAN 7: 4,12,17)

𝒯he Lion symbolizes Babylon, the same as the head of gold on the image of Dan 2:38-46. This is clear from the fact that the four beasts symbolize four kingdoms from Daniel's day on to the eternal kingdom of God (Dan 7: 17-25). The vision was seen during the reign of Belshazzar king of Babylon, and the first beast would naturally represent this kingdom that was in existence when Daniel saw the vision, just as this was true in the first kingdom represented by the metals of the image in Dan 2:38-46. The wings on the lion symbolize the swiftness of the conquests chaldeans as stated in Hab 1: 6-8; Ezek 17: 1-24. The wings were plucked and the lion stood on its feet as a man, which mean that Babylon was no longer was as a lion that could rush upon its prey like an eagle and devour it. A man's heart-weak and faint-took the place of a lion's strength. such was the case of Babylon at the end when she was given over to wealth and luxury as seen in Dan 5: Babylon is also pictured as a lion in Jer 4: 7, CH 50: 17,43-44. Since the first beast represent Babylon, the other three naturally represent Medo-persia, Greece, and Rome that succeed Babylon.

## (THE BEAR, DAN 7: 5,12,17)

𝒯he Bear Symbolizes Mido-persia the same as the silver in the image of Dan 2: It raised itself up on one side representing the greater military strength and influence of the persians. The three ribs in its mouth represent the Mido-persian conquest of Lydia, Babylon, and Egypt. This kingdom of Mido-persia is mentioned in Dan 5:24-31, CH 6: 1-28, CH 7: 5,17, CH 8:1-4f2O; CH 10:1-20, CH 11: 1-2, ISA 13:17-22f CH 21:2, 2 kings 17:6, CH 18:11, Esther 2:6,

## THE LEOPARD, DAN 7: 6,12,17

The Leopard symbolizes Rome the same as the iron in the image of DAN 2: It had four wings of a fowl representing the swiftness of the conquest of Alexander, therein being similar to the Lion. It also had four heads which represent the four divisions of the Empire after the death of Alexander, as we shall see below. This kingdom is mentioned in DAN 2: 32, 35, 39, 45, CH 7:6,17; CH 8:5-25, CH 10:20; CH 11:3-45; Zech 8:13.

## THE BEAST WITHOUT DESCRIPTION DAN 7:7-8,17-27

This beast Symbolizes Rome the same as the iron in the image of DAN 2: It had great iron teeth and was very strong because it broke in pieces all the beast that were before it. It had ten horns and later on another little horn was grown making (eleven altogether DAN 7:23-'24) This little horn had eyes like the eyes of a man and speak very great things DAN 7:7-8, 19-24). The beast itself Symbolizes the old Roman Empire (DAN 7: 7-8,23-24; The ten horns and the little horn symbolize different truth as we shall see.

## THE TEN HORNS, DAN 7: 7-8,17-27

The ten horns symbolize ten kingdoms out of the territory of the old Roman Empire that shall arise in the last days and will be in existence at the time of the second coming of christ. The ten horns will make the fifth kingdom dealt with in this chapter. They correspond to the ten toes on the image of DAN 2: and the ten horns on the beast and dragon in Rev 12: 3, CH 13:1-4, CH 17: 8-17, for they all exist at the same time and are destroyed the same way and by the same person.

## DANIEL VISION OF THE RAM AND THE HE-GOAT (DAN 8)

This vision deals with only two of the kingdoms symbolized in the metals on the image of Dan 2: and by the four beast of Dan 7.-the medo-persian and the Greecian. The purpose of this vision is to narrow down the place where the little horn or Antichrist will be coming from, geographically, from the ten kingdoms to four of the kingdoms, and reveal that his kingdom will be the revived Greecian Empire instead of the Revised Roman Empire. The ANTICHRIST is seen in this chapter as coming out of one of the four Greecian divisions, so we can eliminate entirely the other six of the Revised Roman Empire as being the countries from which the Antichrist will be coming from. IN Dan 7: he is seen coming out of the ten kingdoms of the Revised Roman Empire;

He uses the kingdom that he come out of, to overthrow three others which are the other three divisions of Greece. IN this way he revives the Greecian Empire by coming out of its divisions and overthrowing the other three. THE six kingdoms of the revised Empire which were never a part of Greecian will submit to him, and his kingdom will then become the eighth of Rev 17:8-17, which immediately succeeds the seventh or Revised Rome, but will be destroyed by christ at his coming. The Antichrist arises at beginning of the seventieth week of Daniel 9: 24 and in three and one half years conquers and gain control of all ten kingdoms which he will rule for the last three and one half years of the seventieth week. ALL the kings will continue to rule under him, but as subordinate kings during his short reign.

The vision of the ram and the he-goat is given in DAN 8:1-18, and interpreted in v19-27. Such expressions at the time of the end shall be the vision ... the last of the indignation ... the end shall be ... the latter time of their kingdom... stand up against the prince of princes; but he shall be broken without hand" prove that the vision concerns the days just before the coming of christ to earth.

## WHAT IS THE MEANING OF THE RAM?

$\mathcal{D}$AN 8:1-4,20

The ram symbolizes the Medo-persian Empire the same as the silver in the image of DAN 2: and the bear of DAN 7: it had two horns corresponding to the two arms on the image of DAN 2: and represents the two leaders of the Empire, Darius the Median, and Cyrus the persian. The ram did according to its own will for a period but at the height of his power an he-goat came from the west and destroyed the ram, representing the conquests of Medopersia by Greece.

## THE HE-GOAT, DAN 8:5-26

$\mathcal{T}$he he-goat symbolizes the Greecian Empire the same as the brass in the image of DAN 2: and the leopard in DAN 7: He came from the face of the west and touched not the ground as he went, representing the swiftness of Alexander's conquests. The he-goat had a notable horn between the eyes, representing the first king, which was Alexander the Great. The notable horn was broken, (meaning Alexander died) and in its place there came up four notable horns toward the four winds of heaven, representing the four divisions of the Greecian Empire.

## WHAT ARE THE FOUR DIVISIONS OF GREECE

$\mathcal{T}$he prophet Daniel predicted that the third or the Greecian Empire would be divided into four parts (DAN 8:8,9,21-23 CH 11: 4). This was fulfilled after the death of ALexander the great when four of his generals seized upon his Empire as follows.

1 Cassander took Greece and Macedon
2 Lysimachus took ASIA Minor or present Turkey and Thrace
3 Seleucus took all the eastern parts of the Empire including the modern states of Syria, Iraq, and Iran.

❖  ❖  ❖  ❖  ❖  ❖  ❖  ❖  ❖  ❖  ❖  ❖  ❖  ❖  ❖  ❖  ❖  ❖

4 Ptolemy took the kingdom of Egypt-palestine became a buffer state between Syria and Egypt who waged war with each other for about 150 years ending in 165 B.C. with the reign of Antiochus Epiphanes,king of Syria.

All these divisions except the extreme eastern part of the kingdom of Seluecus were conquered by the Romans and they became part of the old Roman Empire. These four divisions of Greece will become four of the ten kingdoms that will be formed inside the old Roman Empire in the last days.

## WHAT COUNTRY THE ANTICHRIST WILL BE COMING FROM?

The prophet Daniel saw the little horn coming out of one of the four divisions of the Greecian Empire (Dan 8:8-9,21-23).

He said, and out of one of them came forth the little horn, which waxed exceeding great, toward the south, and toward the east, and toward the pleasant land.' This was to be in the latter time of their kingdom" and it must yet be in the future for these kingdom still exist (Dah 8: 23).

These four divisions are known today as Greece, Turkey, Syria, and Egypt. IN DAN 7: We have the Antichrist coming from ten kingdoms inside the Roman Empire and if we did not have the vision of DAN 8: we could believe that he could come from England, Belgium, France, Switzerland, Spain, Portugal, Italy, Austria, Hungary, or some other part of the Old Roman Empire outside of the four divisions of the Greecian Empire. but since we have Dan 8: this vision narrow down the Antichrist from ten kingdoms to four of the ten and definitely limiting his coming from either Greece, Turkey, Syria, or Egypt, for this reason we must limit his coming from one of these four countries.

IF the Antichrist will be coming from either Greece, Turkey, Syria, or Egypt, then it is definite that cannot come from Italy, the Vatican, England, Germany, Russia or any other country of the world, as people have been teaching in the past for years. Therefore, all other speculations of the past are to be thrown into the trash can. Likewise the present speculation that the pope, or some man is the Antichrist is also unscriptural.

This much is clear, that no one knows who the Antichrist will be for he has not yet come and cannot come until after the ten kingdoms are formed inside the Old Roman Empire and until after the rapture of the church, as I have said before.

It is also clear that the Antichrist cannot be any one in past history, because he will be coming from one of the four divisions of the Greecian Empire, which is either Syria, Greece, Turkey, and Egypt. These facts automatically eliminate all modern teachings that Antichrist will come from Italy, Russia, Germany, or from some where else. Antichrist will not come from any one of these countries nor will he reign from the capitals of any one of these countries. The European Union is doing a great job putting things together to fulfill prophecy. God is responsible for prophecy, the prophet is only a spokes man to deliver the message that the Lord give to them so no one will be able to teach it away or preach it away. Ladies and gentlemen it is later than you think, prophecy is sure.

### DID YOU KNOW THAT KING DAVID WILL REIGN AGAIN OVER ALL OF THE HOUSE OF ISRAEL FOR EVER

(A SONG) One night I was in a vision hearing the voice of an angel singing this beautiful song.

David shall reign in majesty, David shall reign in majesty, for the host of hell cannot prevail, David shall reign in majesty.

IF the Lord said so then that is the way it is going to be. This will be true in the millennium and all the ages after. There are a number of passages which mention of David as being resurrected from the dead to reign again over all Israel (Jer 30: v9, But they shall serve the Lord their God, and David their king, whom I will raise up unto them. Ezek 34: 23-24, And I will set one shepherd over them, and he shall feed them, even my servant David he shall feed them, and he shall be their shepherd. v24, And I the Lord will be their God, and my servant David a prince among them; I the Lord have spoken it.

Ezek 37: 24-28, And David my servant shall be king over them; and they shall have one shepherd, they shall also walk in my judgments, and observe my statues and do them. v25, And they shall dwell in the land that I have given unto Jacob my servant, wherein your fathers have dwelt; and they shall dwell therein, even they, and their children, and their children's children for ever; and my servant David shall be prince for ever. v26, moreover I will make a covenant of peace with them, it shall be an everlasting covenant with them; and I will place them, and multiply them, and will set my sanctuary in the midst of them for evermore. v27, my tabernacle also shall be with them; yea, I will be their God, and they shall be my people. v28, And the heathen shall know that I the Lord sanctify Israel, when my sanctuary shall be in the midst of them for evermore.

Hosea 3: 4-5, For the children of Israel shall abide many days without a king, and without a prince and without a sacrifice, and without an image, and without an ephod and without teraphim. v5, Afterward shall the children of Israel return and seek the Lord their God, and David their king, and shall fear the Lord and his goodness in the latter days.

This proves that David will have a higher position when Jesus comes and setup his eternal kingdom here on earth than the twelve apostles because they will have only one tribe each (Luke 22: 28-30) Jesus said to his apostles) ye are they which have continued with me in my temptations.

v29, And I appoint unto you a kingdom, as my father hath appointed unto me. v30, That ye may eat and drink at my table in my kingdom, and sit on thrones judging the twelve tribes of Israel.

Jesus will be Lord over David and all other kings and priest

Of that period. Jesus will be king of kings and Lord of Lords Rev 17:v14, Rev 19: 12,16).

I did not compose this song, I tell it to you just the way I receive, the Lord telling me the same thing that he told the prophets thousands of years ago, but this time he tell it to me in the form of a song, the Lord want me to know that he stand by his word and that satan and his host cannot prevail.

I have listen to great singers singing the songs of zion and if it was possible I would live in that atmosphere for the rest of my life, but if these great singers want to learn how to sing they need to go to the school angels to learn how to sing. I can say so because I heard them sing many times in my visions, their voices are like music in itself, they truly are.

## THIS IS ANOTHER SONG I HEARD IN A NIGHT VISION

(A SONG) It will be joy, joy, forever upon the crystal shore, It will be joy, joy, forever upon the crystal shore, when all the saints shall gather to hear well done, it will be joy, joy, forever upon the crystal chore.

The Lord is my witness I did not compose this song, I did not add one word to it, I write it just the way the Lord gave it to me. IN ISAIAH 35: v10, the prophet speak of this joy, the prophet said, And the ransomed of the Lord shall return, and come to zion with songs and everlasting joy upon their heads; they shall obtain joy and gladness, and sorrow and sighing shall flee away.

IN matt 25: Jesus speak a parable and said in v14, For the kingdom of heaven is as a man travelling into a far country, who called his own servants, and delivered unto them his goods. v15, To one servant he gave five talents, to another he gave two talents, and to another he gave one talent, and went his way. The servant that received five talents traded with it and gain five more, also the servant with the two talents gain two more. So in v2l Jesus said His Lord said unto them well done, thou good and faithful servant, thou hast been faithful over a few things, I will make thee ruler over many things, enter thou into the joy of thy Lord.

But the servant that received the one talent see things differently. v24, He said his Lord was a hard man, who want to reap where he did not sown, and gather where thou hast not strawed. v25,He said he was afraid, and went and hid his talent in the earth. But his excuse was not good enough. v26, His Lord answered and said unto him, thou wicked and slothful servant. v28 His talent was taken away from him and given to the one that had ten talents. so use your talent for the Lord to the best of your ability and do it with joy.

The attitude of a slothful person is one who think what others do prospers where it would fail in his case. Another characteristic of a slothful person is one who always afraid to venture out in business and take risks.

## A VISION OF A GREAT DRAGON CAME UP FROM UNDER THE EARTH

It was in the year 1965, one night I had this vision, the Lord showed me a great dragon came up from under the earth. I saw a certain part of the earth start cracking up may be about 30 feet from where I was standing, I realize something very large was coming up from under the ground, no one know that such a large and dangerous creature was living just under our feet, it was a fearful and shocking sight. I could see the back of a very large dark colored creature coming up, so I became very fearful and I ran and climb a very tall coconut tree and watch the creature from up there. This creature was a very large dragon looking more like a crocodile but about twenty times bigger than the largest crocodile that ever lived, It was very tall, with a very long tail. It was a very dreadful looking creature. The dragon walk pass the coconut tree but did not looked up, and thank God for that, if that dragon had looked up I would be its first meal because I was in its reach.

This dragon is the devil, in Rev 12:v9 John said, And the

great dragon was cast out, that old serpent, called the devil, and satan, which deceiveth the whole world; he was cast out into the earth, and his angels were cast out with him. John said he was cast out into into the earth, I saw this great dragon came up from under the earth, meaning that he is living among humanity destroying the nations and they are not aware of him, they are not conscious of knowing that the devil or satan is deceiving and destroying them.

This vision is the same as that of John in Rev 12:v9. God's people are not ignorant-of the devices of the devil because we are no more in darkness. IN 2 Cor 2: v10-11, Paul said we must always forgive one another lest satan should get an advantage of us. IN Eph 4: 26-27, Paul said, Be Ye angry and sin not, let not the sun go down upon your warth. v27 Neither give place to the devil.

Believers in christ must be watchful at all times so that the devil do not get a foothold in their lives, because if he get one foot he will take ten feet and will not be satisfied until he destroyed that believer.

## A VISION OF A SERPENT OUT OF THIS WORLD

This is another description of the devil, it is amazing what dreams can reveal. I dream that I was travelling on a very lonely road, I could see that not many people travel on that road, I kept going until I met two preachers who was well known to me. we stopped and we talked for a while, after I leave and was walking for about minute, then I saw a very large serpent running coming toward me, so I was lifted up off the earth and in the air, the serpent looked up at me but could not reach me.

The serpent was going in the direction of the preachers, so I was hoping that they would see the serpent coming because it could creep up on them from behind. This was no ordinary serpent, it was very large and of a very fearful and vicious appearance, the appearance of this creature would send pack of lions fleeing for

❖ ❖ ❖ ❖ ❖ ❖ ❖ ❖ ❖ ❖ ❖ ❖ ❖ ❖ ❖ ❖ ❖

their lives. Serpents do not have feet, but this one had two front feet, short, thick, and strong, which tells me that the serpent did have at least two feet at one point before it was cursed-IN GEN 3: after the serpent cause Adam and Eve to sin the Lord curse the serpent. v14, And the Lord said unto the serpent, because thou hast done this, thou art cursed above all cattle, and above every beast of the field, upon thy belly shalt thou go, and dust shalt thou eat all the days of thy life.

This serpent ran very fast for its size, the two front feet were short, thick, and strong, this serpent had a jugular under its neck like that of a cow, and it swing side to side as it ran. This serpent had a mane from the back of the head down to its tail, and it was raised like that of an angry dog but much higher. This was a very large serpent with a body about twenty feet long or more. This fearful and angry looking serpent represent the vicious nature of the devil. Jesus said the devil come to steal, to kill and to destroy, but I am come that you may have life and have it more abundantly.

## WHAT THE IS DEVIL IS ACCORDING TO THE BIBLE

The Bible makes it abundantly clear what the devil is, and answers any question one could ask about him that needs to be known. The devil is a real person just like any other angel and will remain to be so; personal statements in scripture prove that he is a person. IN lchron 21: v1, we read, And satan stood up against Israel, and provoked David to number Israel. And that create a very big problem for David because the Lord was angry with David, because the Lord did not tell David to number Israel.

## THE LORD OFFERS DAVID A CHOICE OF 3 PUNISHMENTS

v9, And the Lord spake unto Gad, David's seer, saying. v10, Go and tell David saying, thus saith the Lord, I offer thee three things choose thee one of them, that I may do it unto thee. vll, SO Gad,

David seer, said choose thee. v12, Either three years of famine, or three months to be destroyed before thy foes, while that the sword of thine enemies overtaketh thee, or else three days of the sword of the Lord, even the pestilence in the land, and the angel of the Lord destroying throughout all the coast of Israel. Now therefore advise thyself what word I shall bring again to him that sent me.

## DAVID CHOOSE TO FALL INTO THE HAND OF THE LORD

*V*13, And David said unto Gad, I am in great strait, let me fall into the hand of the Lord, for very great are his mercies, but let me not fall into the hand of man. This one act of satan cost Israel 70,000 men. David said what any sensible person would say who know God and his dealings. The king choose the last of three offers, three days of pestilence, preferring to fall into the hands of the Lord whose mercies are great, and not into the hands of men who show no mercy.

IN less than three days 70,000 men died of the plague. How many more would have perished if David had taken any of the other two offers? cannot be estimated, but no doubt many more than what the pestilence did, and the suffering would last much longer, David had been in the hands of king Saul for years and later on he had to flee from Absalom his own son, so David could not make that mistake again, so he cast himself upon the mercies of God, v13. So we can see from this passage that satan is a real person and can cause serious problems.

Satan has access to heaven according to Job 1: 6-12, CH 2:1-7, Rev 12: 7-12 satan stands up against people to resist them as any other person can, Zech 3: 1-2, And he shewed me Joshua the high priest standing before the angel of the Lord, and satan standing at his right hand to resist him. v2 And the Lord said unto satan, the Lord rebuke thee, O satan; even the Lord that hath chosen Jerusalem rebuke thee; is not this a brand plucked out of the fire? 1 Peter 5: 8-9 Be sober, vigilant, (watchful) because your adversary the devil, as a roaring lion, walking about, seeking whom he may devour. v9 whom resist steadfast in the faith, knowing that the same afflictions are accomplished in your brethren that are in the world. see PSALMS 109: v6)

Jesus dealt with him as with a person. IN the temptation satan tested christ for forty days before he was Dermanently dismissed Matt 4: 1-11, Luke 4: 1-13) Jess, waged war on satan as on a person. He went about destroying the works of the devil and delivering men from his power (1 John 3:v8, Acts 10: v38, How God anointed Jesus of Nazareth with the Holy Ghost and with power; who went about doing good, and healing all that were oppressed of the devil, for God was with him Luke 13: 16). Jesus taught that satan was a real person. He said that he had seen him fallen from heaven (Luke 10:v18) and that he was a deceiver of the whole world and the personal leader of many angels (Rev 12: 7-12) and that he will give his power to Antichrist and receive personal worship.(Rev 13: 1-4) And that he will at fight at Armageddon and will be taken and bound in chain and into prison for 1.000 years (Rev 20: 1-3).

And that he will let out of prison and lead one more rebellion against God and then he will be cast into the lake of fire to be tormented forever (Rev 20: 7-10). The apostles fought with satan as with a real person; "we wrestle not against flesh and blood, but against principalities, against powers, against the rulers of the darkness of this world, against spiritual wickedness in high places (Eph 6: 10-18). ON one occasion the apostle Paul wanted to go to thessalonica but he could not, he said satan hindered us (l Thess 2: v18). The apostle Peter referred to satan as an "adversary, and as a roaring lion, walking about, seeking whom he may devour (l Peter 5: 8-9).

The apostles warned men against a personal devil and told saints not to give any place to the devil, and to stand against the wiles of the devil ... Resist the devil and he will flee Eph 4:27, CH 6: 11, Jas 4: 7, 1 Peter 5: 8-9, statements of this kind could refer only to a person. Since satan or devil is a person he must be treated as a person, we say no to him and yes to Jesus christ, the one who called us out of darkness into his marvelous light.

Why know the truth and do the wrong thing? IF you are free then stay free and be not entangled again in the yoke of bondage Gal 5: v1, we are at war with Satan so fight to win, one cannot lost their will to fight and expect to win so fight the good fight of faith and lay hold on eternal life, where unto thou art also called 1 Tim 6: 12.

He is mentioned in scripture over 175 times by many names-Lucifer (ISA 14: 12-14); Devil and Satan (Rev 12: 9); Beelzebub (Matt 10:25; CH 12; 24) Belial (2 Cor 6:15); Adversary (I Peter 5: 8-9); Dragon(12:3-12; CH 13:1-4; CH 20: 1-3); Serpent (2 Cor 11: 3; Rev 12: 9); the God of this world (2 Cor 4: 4);the prince of the power of the air (Eph 2: 1-3) the accuser of the brethren (Rev 12: 10); the enemy (Matt 13: 39); tempter (Matt 4:3); the wicked one (Matt 13:19,38) and that wicked one (1 John 5: 18).

Satan is an angel with a body, soul, and like all other angels. He is described as a most beautiful creature who fell through personal pride over his own beauty (Ezek 28: 11-17, 1 Tim 3: 6); He has seen with a body 1 Chron 21: 1, Job 1: 6-12, CH 2: 1-7, and many other scripture.

THE DREAMER: I can testify to that because I have seen the devil for myself in visions with a body just like a human body with a head, two eyes, mouth, two hands, and feet, he talk with me about coming back to him, I told him he did not create me, I said to him the Lord create me and will I serve, so the scripture are true, the devil is a person and he do has a body. I saw him on other occasion and he talk with me concerning three people that were healed a week before, he threaten me and walked away, so he is a person. I saw him again on another occasion in my vision and he want me to do things for him and when I refuse he pull his sword on me and swipe at me, so he is a person like all other angels that has a body, and whosoever that do not believe that there is a real devil will be the next victim.

❖ ❖ ❖ ❖ ❖ ❖ ❖ ❖ ❖ ❖ ❖ ❖ ❖ ❖ ❖ ❖

Satan is a great celestial and terrestrial ruler, in Eph 2:v2, Paul said, Wherein in time past ye walk according to the course of this world, according to the prince of the power of the air, the spirit that now worketh in the children of disobedience. Eph 6: 10-18, 2 Cor 4: v4, Paul said, IN whom the god of this world hath blinded the minds of them which believe not, lest the light of the glorious gospel of christ, who is the image of God should shine unto them. John 12: 31) Jesus said, Now is the judgment of this world: now shall the prince of this world be cast out. Satan is ruling in business, social, political, and religious activities of the majority of mankind.

The realm of satan is divided into organized principalities and powers in the heavenlies Eph 6: 10-12, Finally, my brethren be strong in the Lord, and in the power of his might. vll, put on the whole armor of God, that ye may be able to stand against the wiles of the devil. v12, For we wrestle not against flesh and blood, but against principalities, against powers, against the rulers of the darkness of this world, against spiritual wickedness in high places. Matt 12: 24-30) and other scripture. Those that he controlled are fallen angels, and fallen men, and demons of various kinds (Matt 25: 41, Rev 12: 7-12, John 8: 44, 1 John 3: 8-10; JAMES 2:v19, Thou believest that there is one God; thou doest well; the devil also believe and tremble. Satan is the head of man's religion and is the leader in many religious affairs Rev 2:v9, I know thy works, and tribulation, and poverty, but thou art rich) and I know the blasphemy of them which say they are Jews, "and are not, but are synagogue of satan. CH 3:v9, 2 Cor 11: 14-15, And no marvel; for satan himself is transformed into an angel of light. v15, Therefore it is no great thing if his ministers also be transformed as the ministers of righteousness; whose end shall be according to their works.

## SATAN IS A MIGHTY ANGEL AND CANNOT BE TAKEN LIGHTLY

*O*ur Lord Jesus christ defeat him at the cross and give us-power over him, Jesus called him a strong man, but greater is in you than he that is in the world (1 John 4:v4) the devil cannot be taken lightly. Believers in christ must seek to be filled with the anointing power of the holy spirit on their lives in order to stand. Paul said, Finally my brethren, be strong in the Lord, and in the power of his might. put on the whole armor of God, that ye may be able to stand against the wiles of the devil.

For we wrestle not against flesh and blood, but against principalities against powers against the rulers of the darkness of this world, against spiritual wickedness in high places. Wherefore take unto you the whole armor of God, that ye may be able to withstand in the evil day, and having done all to stand Eph 6: 10-13).

The great blessings of the armor of the Lord is that it gives one the ability to stand against all enemies. The ability to withstand all attacks, the ability to quench every fiery darts of satan. The devil uses method and plans to deceive, entrap enslave, and ruin the souls of man. A man's method of sinning is the devil's method of damning the soul. IN view of the fact that you have such enemies be endued with or clothed with the armor of the Lord, it will make you victorious.

## SATAN IS THE PRINCE OF THE POWER OF THE AIR

*I*N Eph 2:v2 Paul called him the prince of the power of the air. v2 Where in time past ye walked according to the course of this world, according to the prince of the power of the air the spirit that now worketh in the children of disobedience. This world is satan domain he rules here, this is where he demonstrate his power, he is the god of this world and without the power of God in our lives we will not be able to overcome. This is in reality of the old man of the scripture that works in the children of disobedience

Rom 6: v6, Knowing this that our old man is crucified with him, that the body of sin might be destroyed, that henceforth we should not serve sin.

For those who are living sinful lives Jesus said, ye are of your father the devil, and the lusts of your father ye will do, He was a murderer from the beginning, and abode not in the truth because there is no truth in him. When he speaketh a lie, he speaeth of his own: for he is a liar, and the father of it John 8:44. He that committeth sin is of the devil: for the devil sinneth from the beginning, for this purpose the son of God was manifested, that he might destroy the works of the devil (1 John 3:v8). CH 5: 18). Satan is the prince or ruler of the air, because in this realm the evil spirit dwell, all of whom that are under his dominion.

When a person get rid of this evil spirit out of their lives by accepting christ as Lord of their lives they no longer have the old man dominating them, they are no more under his control. Because if any man be in christ he is a new creature, old things are passed away, behold, all things are become new. And all things are of God, who hath reconciled us unto himself by Jesus christ, and hath given to us the ministry of reconciliation. To wit that God was in christ reconciling the world unto himself, not imputing their trespasses unto them; and hath committed unto us the word of reconciliation (2 Cor 5: 17-19).

## AN ANGELIC VISITOR

$\mathcal{D}$aniel 10: IN the year of Cyrus king of Persia a thing was revealed unto Daniel, Daniel was fasting and praying for three weeks, he did not ate bread, no flesh nor wine, neither did he anoint himself until three whole weeks were fulfilled v1-3. Then he had an angelic visitor. He was of a very great and glorious appearance.

Then I lifted up mine eyes, and looked, and behold a certain man clothed in linen, whose loins were girded with fine gold of u'phaz. His body also was like the beryl, (its a beautiful stone) and his face as the appearance of lightning, and his eyes as lamps of fire, and his arms and feet like in colour to polished brass, and his voice of his words like the voice of a multitude. v5-6). This vision was in real life, it was not a dream, but his presence was so impressive that the effect cause Daniel to lost all strength and he fell into a deep sleep on his face on the ground. this is a long time for a man to be on fasting and prayer, and constant emotional strain, this is the same as saying that he was on a total fast.

## SATAN IS ORGANIZED AND MEAN BUSINESS

*H*ere is an example of prayer being delayed (v12-13) but such delay should never hinder faith or cause one to give up seeking God. Daniel prayer was answered, but something went wrong, the angel Gabriel that was carrying the message to Daniel was detained by the angelic forces of satan over persia. IN v13, Gabriel told Daniel, But the prince of the kingdom of persia withstood me one and twenty days: but, Lo, Michael one of the chief princes, came to help me, and I remained there with the kings of persia. This should only urge one to renew one's effort and to hold on in prayer and faith until the answer is realized (Luke 18:1-8). Gabriel said, I am come to answer to the prayer that you have prayed.

## A SATANIC PRINCE

*T*his is a satanic prince or ruler of the kingdom of persia, This is a mighty angel one who ruling the kingdom of persia for satan who is known in scripture as being the God of this world, one who having authority over man's dominion, Matt 4: 8-9, Again, the devil taketh him up into an exceeding high mountain, and sheweth him all the kingdoms of the world, and the glory of them. And saith unto him, All these things will I give thee, if thou wilt fall down and worship me. CH 12: 24-30, John 8:44, CH 12:31,2 Cor 4:4, Eph 2:2, CH 6:10-18, 1 John 3:8, Rev 12: 7-12, CH 16:13-16, CH 20: 1-10).

Over all the governments of this world satan has his trusted angels who are responsible to him to carrying out his will in these governments. He seeks to hinder God's plan in the fulfillment of prophecy regarding world kingdoms.

God also has trusted angels and they carry out his will concerning what he has predicted to take place in the kingdoms of the world Dan 10: 11-21, CH ll:v1, CH 12:v1). There are wars between these two groups of angels in the heavenlies v13, 20-21, CH ll:v1, CH 12:v1, Jude v9, Rev 12:7-12). All wars lost or won on earth are the result of wars lost or won by these heavenly armies. Not only over every government of this world are good and evil spirit beings seeking to influence and carry out the will of their masters, but also over every individual life the same is true(Matt 18:10, 2 Cor 10: 4-6, Eph 2: 2, CH 6: 10-18, Heb 1:14, Jude v9). Satan himself is very active along with those evil spirits seeking to defeat God's purpose in the lives of his children (l Chron 21: v1, job 1:v6, CH 2: v1, Zech 3:v1, Matt 4: 1-11, 2 Cbr 4:v4, Eph 2:v2, CH 6: 10-18, Rev 12: 12). Michael is the prince of Israel. Satan is an enemy and must be treated as such by God's people, we are at war with him. And they overcame him by the blood of the lamb, and by the word of their testimony; and they loved not their lives unto death Rev 12:11).

Therefore rejoice ye heavens and ye that dwell in them, woe to the inhabiters of the earth and of the sea! for the devil is come down unto you, having great wrath, because he knoweth that he hath but a short time (Rev 12:11-12). our adversary, meaning one who take a stand against the other, and he take a stand against both God and man.

## THE WAR OF SATAN ON THE SAINTS

One of the most important work of-the devil now among men is to counterfeit the doctrines and experiences of God as revealed in scripture in order to deceive the saints.

God's people are commanded to prove and test all doctrines

and experience in the supernatural realm to see if they are of god or of satan. (2 Cor 2: 12-16, Now we have received, not the spirit of the world, but the spirit which is of God, that we might know the things that are freely given to us of God. v13, which things also we speak, not in the words which man's wisdom teacheth, but which the Holy Ghost, comparing spiritual things with spiritual. v14, But the natural man receiveth not the things of the spirit of God; for they are foolishness unto him, neither can he know them, because they are spiritually discerned. v15, but he that is spiritual judgeth all things yet he himself is judged of no man. v16, For who hath known the mind of the Lord that he may instruct him? but we have the mind of christ.

Phil 1:9-10, And this I pray, that your love may abound yet more and more in knowledge and in all judgment; v10, That ye may approve things that are excellent; that ye may be sincere and without offense till the day of christ;) 1 Thess 5: 21-22, Prove all things; hold fast that which is good. Obstain from all appearance of evil.

IN 1 John 4: 1-6, John said, BELOVED, believe not every spirit, but try the spirits whether they are of God, because many false prophets are gone out into the world. (HOW TO TEST THE SPIRIT) v2 Hereby know ye the spirit of God; every spirit that confesseth that Jesus Christ is come in the flesh is of God. v3, And every spirit that confesseth not that Jesus Christ is come in the flesh is not of God. (HOW TO OVERCOME DEMONS) v4, Ye are of God little children, and have overcome them: because greater is he that is in you, than he that is in the world. v5, They are of the world, therefore speak they of the world, and the world heareth them. v6, We are of God; he that knoweth God heareth us; he that is not of God heareth not us. Hereby know we the spirit truth, and the spirit of error.

It is certain that not every religion, doctrine, and experience among men are of God, so we must judge them by the written word of God.

One of the greatest danger for spiritual believers in christ is

✧ ✧ ✧ ✧ ✧ ✧ ✧ ✧ ✧ ✧ ✧ ✧ ✧ ✧ ✧ ✧ ✧

to accept any thing and everything in the realm of the supernatural as being from God. Not because the believer is a child of God that does not stop the devil from trying in every conceivable way to imitate God to deceive the believers in christ. In fact, believers in christ are the ones he concentrates on and wars against.

## THE MINISTERS OF SATAN IN PLAIN SIGHT CAN YOU RECOGNIZE THEM?

*D*o you become a member of a church because they said they believe in God and preach from the Bible? the Bible teaches that the devil also believe and tremble James 2: 19, the devil also use the word of God, he tried it on Jesus and lost. Matt 4:5-6, Then the devil taketh him up into the holy city, and setteth him on a pinnacle of the temple, v6 And saith unto him, if thou be the son of God, cast thyself down: for it is written, He shall give his angels charge concerning thee: and in their hands they shall bear thee up, lest at any time thou dash thy foot against a stone. God's people must know the Bible for themselves so you can fight the devil and win. The ministers of satan do not believe the whole Bible they pick and choose what to believe, such rights are not given to the Christian church, so you know they are not of God.

The apostle said, And no marvel, or don't be amazed, for satan himself is transformed into an angel of light. Therefore it is no great thing if his ministers also be transformed into as the ministers of righteousness, whose end shall be according to their works 2 Cor 11:14-15) This make it very clear that the counterfeit of satan will be substitute for the truth as close to the light and truth as possible to deceive those that are seeking for the truth.

So it is very important that every one that name the name of Christ be very careful about what you believe and what supernatural power they yield themselves to. There are definite ways outlined in scripture by which a person can used to detect what kind of spirit is seeking to control them.

Here are some ways a person can use to detect good and

evil spirits and there operations and doctrines.

(1) Any doctrine that denies or in any way cause doubts and unbelief concerning anything taught in scripture is not of God and is coming from demons. Any religion that denies the inspiration of the Bible; and the reality of God as a person; if they denies the divine sonship of Jesus Christ as the only begotten son of God; if they denies the virgin birth, the pre-existerice of Jesus Christ; if they denies the divinity of Christ and his miraculous power and supernatural ministry; if they denies his death, burial, and bodily resurrection, if they denies that Christ was manifested bodily after his resurrection. IF they denies the bodily ascension of Christ to heaven and that he is coming back to set up a kingdom in this world that will have no end.

IF they denies the reality and power of the Holy Spirit and his ministry among men to convict them of their sin, if they denies that the Holy Spirit empowered men in christ to carry on the work of God among men, if they do not believe in the reality of the Christian experience as being born again, or the new birth, and are cleansed from sin, and are living free from sin, if they denies the healing power of Jesus Christ they are not of God. IF they denies the baptism of the Holy Spirit, miracies and signs following them that believe, and answer to prayer they are not of God.

IF they do not believe that God made man a free moral agent, and that man is free to choose, stay clear of such they are agents of satan the prince of darkness. Satan is the only one that will force a man against his own will not God. Any religion that will hunt you down like a wild dog and kill you because you leave their religion is not of God, the prince of darkness is their God, not the God of Abraham, Isaac, and Jacob.

Any religion that do not believe that one must be born again in order to inherit the kingdom of God according to the scripture is not of God. Any religion that teaches contrary to these and all other fundamental doctrines of scripture is of Satan, design by Satan to damned the soul in eternal hell.

✧  ✧  ✧  ✧  ✧  ✧  ✧  ✧  ✧  ✧  ✧  ✧  ✧  ✧  ✧  ✧  ✧

## MAN HAS LOST THE ABILITY TO TAKE CARE OF HIMSELF

*B*efore Satan showed in the garden of Eden, man was doing fine, they were so sinless they did not know that they were naked, the Lord would come down in the cool of the day and visit man Gen 3:v8, but after Satan showed up in the form Of a serpent and trick them to eat the fruit that they were told not to eat, after they ate the fruit they were not the same any more because the bullet of sin pierce their guiltless innocent spirit and they died. Man do not even have the ability to save himself from himself, if a man cannot save himself from himself it does not get any worse than that.

Sin have driven man to the point that man have lost the will to live so he get himself a gun and killed himself, or he over dose himself, or he blow up himself and said he is going to paradise, ladies and gentlemen this is insanity. man is helpless on his own and the devil know it and use false religion and trap untold millions to believe that they are in the right church. There is not one religion on the planet that can save the soul of man, only through the precious blood of Jesus Christ God son can one be saved and no one else.

The apostle Paul said, This is the stone which was set at naught of you builders, which is become the head of the corner. Neither is there salvation in any other, for there is none other name under heaven given among men, whereby we must be saved Acts 4: 11-12). Jesus said, I am the way, the truth, and the life, no man cometh unto the father, but by me John 14:v6).

## SATAN BLINDED THE MIND

*T*he apostle Paul said, But if our gospel be hid, it is hid to them that are lost: IN whom the God of this world hath blinded the minds of them which believe not, lest the light of the glorious gospel of christ, who is the image of God, should shine unto them. The gospel is hidden from men because they willfully closed their eyes to the gospel as in 2 Cor 3:13-16, Matt 13:14-16, if the heart of any one who hears the gospel is veiled it is clear that he is lost and are under the power of sin and satan.

Those who refuse to hear the gospel are the ones that satan want to work with to continue his work of darkness and hardness of heart 2 Cor 4:3-4, The light of the gospel of Christ shining into our darkened hearts is like the bursting forth of the sunlight in the darkness Gen 1:2. Satan know that the gospel of Christ will free man from his power so he will use every thing he possible can to keep man in darkness.

The power of the gospel is to free men and women from the power of sin and satan. Paul said, Who hath delivered us from the power of darkness, and hath translated us into the kingdom of his dear son Col 1:13) some say it is foolishness, but the foolishness of God is wiser than men, and the weakness of God is stronger than men, l Cor 1: 25).

## IS THERE A DIVINE TRINITY, NAMELY FATHER SON AND HOLY SPIRIT?

*W*hat we mean by Divine Trinity is that there are three separate and distinct persons in the Godhead, each one having his own personal spirit body, personal soul, and personal spirit in the same sense as each human being, angel, or any other being having his own body, soul and spirit, we mean whether a spirit body or a flesh body, the house for the indwelling of the personal soul and spirit. The soul is that which feels and the spirit is that which knows.

The doctrine of the Trinity can be clearly seen, being understood by the visible things that are made, even his eternal power and Godhead; so that they are without excuse (Ron 1:v20). What on earth was created in the image and likeness of God? man (Gen 1:26-28).Do God's image and likeness consist only of moral and spiritual powers? if so, it can be concluded that is only a moral and spiritual being, is God bodiless? if so we conclude that man is bodiless. is man bodiless? the answer is no.

❖ ❖ ❖ ❖ ❖ ❖ ❖ ❖ ❖ ❖ ❖ ❖ ❖ ❖ ❖ ❖

IS God only one being made up of several persons or beings in one being? if so, we can conclude that man is one person or being made up of many. Does God need a flesh body in order to have any kind of body? no! There are such things as spirit and heavenly bodies (1 Cor 15:35-38. From this passage we learn that all thing in creation-grain, fish, birds, beast, man, angels, and even the planets have bodies, size, shapes, and forms. The Bible teaches that God has a body, shape, image, likeness, bodily parts,a personal soul and spirit, and all other things that constitute a being or a person with a body, soul, and spirit. God is a spirit: and they that worship him must worship him in spirit and in truth, John 4:v24, (note John 5: v37).

The Bible teaches of angels, Cherubim, Seraphim, and all other spirit beings that have spirit bodies and personal soul and spirit. They have been seen with the natural eyes of men over 100 times in scripture. The apostle Paul said, Be not forgetful to entertain strangers: for thereby some have entertained angels unawares. IF all other spirit beings have spirit bodies, could not the members of the Trinity also have spirit bodies? From the 284 passages on spirits in scripture prove that spirit bodies are just as real and capable of operating in the material world as flesh and blood beings are.

There is no such thing as a world of creation made up of invisible substance. The so-called spirit-world must be understood simple as spirit beings inhabiting material worlds created by God. Heaven itself is a material planet (Gen 1:v1,Heb 11: 10-16) having cities, mansions, inhabitants, living conditions etc, in heaven.

Heaven is a real place just as this earthly planet is real, I have been to other planet in my vision and it is very real, I also been to heaven in my vision and heaven is a very real place, I saw a very large dragon in heaven, John also saw a red dragon in heaven Rev 12:v3, I saw also a very large white building in heaven, filled with millions of small lights on the inside, I saw gates that leads into the building, I saw streets that leads to the building, so the heaven where God dwells is a real place, it is not invisible, because the planets are not invisible, I also saw people dress in white going into the building.

## GOD HAS BEEN SEEN MANY TIMES WITH HUMAN EYES

$\mathcal{G}$en 18:1-33, Gen 32:24-30, And Jacob was left alone, and there wrestled a man with him until the breaking of the day. v25 And when he saw that he prevailed not against him, he touched the hollow of his thigh, and the hollow of Jacob's thigh was out of joint, as he wrestled with him. v26, And he said, let me go, for the day breaketh. And Jacob said, I will not let thee go, except thou bless me. v27, And he said unto him, what is thy name? and he said, Jacob. v28, And he said, Thy name shall be called no more Jacob but Israel; for as a prince hast thou power with God and with men, and hast prevailed. v29, And Jacob ask him, and said tell me, I pray thee, thy name, and he said, wherefore is it that thou dost ask after my name? and he blessed him there. v30,And Jacob called the name of the place pe-neil, for I have seen God face to face and my life is preserved.

Exod 24: 9-11, Then went up Moses, and Aaron, Naldab, and A-bi-hu, and seventy of the elders of Israel. v10, And they saw the God of Israel; and there was under his feet as it were paved work of a sapphire stone, and as it were the body of heaven in his clearness. vll, And upon the nobles of the children of Israel he laid not his hand, also they saw God, and did eat and drink. Exod 33: 11-23, And the Lord spake unto Moses face to face as a man speaketh unto his friend. And he turned again into the camp, but his servant Joshua, the son of Nun, a young man, departed not out of the tabernacle ...

Josh 5:13-15, And it came to pass, when Joshua was by Jericho, that he lifted up his eyes and looked, and, behold, there stood a man over against him with his sword drawn in his hand and Joshua said unto him, art thou for us, or for our adversaries?

v14, And he said, Nay; but as captain of the host of the Lord am I now come, and Joshua fell on his face to the earth, and did worship, and said unto him, what saith my lord unto his servant? v15, And the captain of the Lord's host said unto Joshua Loose thy shoe from off thy foot; for the place whereon thou standest is holy .And Joshua did so.

Judges 6:11-23, CH 13:3-26, 1 Chron 21:16-17, Job 42:v5, ISA 6: Ezek 1:26-28, Ezek 10:1,20, Ezek 40:v3, Dan 7:9-14, CH 10:5-10, Acts 7:56-59, Rev 4: 2-5, Rev 5:1,5-7,11-14, Rev 6:16, Rev 7: 9-17, and more, There are over 20,000 references about God in scripture we get to know all we need to know about the subject. IF we will take the Bible literally as to what we says about God, as we do with other things the subject will be very clear, but if we make God a mystery, and ignore the plain statements of scripture about God, and refuse to believe the many description of God given by those who have seen one, two, and three separate persons called God, then we will remain in ignorance.

Some people say we serve three Gods but we don't, the unity of the Trinity is so perfect that they are one. Moses said, Hear, o Israel, the Lord our God is one Lord. And thou shalt love the Lord thy God with all thine heart, and with thy soul, and with all thy might Deut 6:4-6. Name of God prove plurality of persons. The hebrew word Elohim is the word for God in Gen 1:1, and in over 2,700 other places in the Old Testament. It is a uniplural noun meaning Gods and is so translated 239 times (Gen 3:v5, For God doeth know that in the day ye eat thereof, then your eyes shall be opened, and ye shall be as God's knowing good and evil.

Exod 22:28, Thou shalt not revile the Gods, nor curse the ruler of thy people. 1 SAM 4:8, Woe unto us! who shall deliver us out of the hand of these mighty "Gods? these are the Gods that smote the Egyptians with all the plagues in the wilderness.

Dan 2:11, And it is a rare thing that the king requireth, and there is none other that can shew it before the king, except the Gods, whose dwelling is not with flesh. Dan 4:6-9, Therefore made

I a decree to bring in all the wise men of Babylon before me, that they might make known unto me the interpretation of the dream. v7, Then came in the magicians, the astrologers, the chal-de-ans, and the soothsayers, and I told the dream before them, but they did not make known unto me the interpretation thereof. v8, But at the last Daniel came in before me whose name was Belte-shaz-zar, according to the name of my God, and in whom is the spirit of the holy Gods, and before him I told the dream, saying. v9, o Bel-thee-shazzar master of the magicians, because I know that the spirit of the holy Gods is in thee, and no secret trobleth thee, tell me the visions of my dream that I have seen, and the interpretation thereof.

Dan 5:11,14, There is a man in thy kingdom, in whom is the spirit of the holy Gods, and in the days of thy father light and understanding and wisdom, like the wisdom of the Gods, was found in him, whom the king Nub-u-chad-hezzar thy father, the king, I say, thy father, made master of the magicians, astrologers, chal-de-tins and soothsayers; v14, I have even heard of thee, that the spirit of the Gods is in thee and that and light and understanding and excellent wisdom is found in thee etc.)

Sometimes Elohim is used with plural verbs and pronduns, the Gods they caused me to wonder Gen 20:13) and there the Gods they appeared unto me (Gen 35:7) plural pronouns are used of GOd. proving plurality of persons Gen 1:26 And God said, let us make man in our image, after our likeness, and let them have dominion over the fish of the sea, and over the fowl of the air, and over the cattle, and over all the earth, and over every creeping thing that creepeth upon the earth.

Gen 3:22, And the Lord God said, behold, the man is become as one of us, to know good and evil; and now, lest he put forth his hand, and take also of the tree of life and eat it and live forever. Gen 11:7, Go to,let us go down, and there confound their language, that they may not understand one another's speech. ISA 6:8, Also I heard the voice of the Lord, saying, whom shall I send and who will go for us? Then said I, here am I; send me. John 14:23, Jesus answered and said unto him if a man love me, he will keep my words and my father will love him and we will come unto him, and make our abode with him, (John 17:11,22-23, And now I no more in the world, but these are in the world, and I come to thee, Holy father, keep through thine own name those whom thou hast given me, that they may be one, as we are one.

v22, And the glory which thou gavest me I have given them; that they may be one, even as we are one. v23, I in them, and thou in me, that they may be made perfect in one; and that the world may know that thou hast sent me, and hast loved them, as thou hast loved me.

First, second, and third personal pronouns are used hundreds of times in scripture, referring to one, two, and three persons of the Godhead in the same sense they are used of men. Sometimes the different member of the Deity them to and of one another in the same sense man uses them.

IN John 17 alone Jesus uses them 162 times in speaking to and of his father. John 14: 16-17, And I will pray the father, and he shall give you another comforter, that he may abide with you forever,v17, Even the spirit of truth, whom the world cannot receive, because it seeth him not, neither knoweth him; but ye know him, for he dwelleth with you, and shall be in you. v26, But the comforter, which is the Holy Ghost, whom the father will send in my name, he shall teach you all things, and bring all things to your remembrance, whatsoever I have said unto you.

John 15:26, But when the comforter is come, whom I will send unto you from the father, even the spirit of truth, which proceedeth from the father, he shall testify of me.

John 16:7-I5, Nevertheless I tell you the truth; it is expedient for you that I go away, for if I go not away, the comforter will not come unto you, but if I depart, I will send him unto you. v8, And when he is come, he will reprove the world of sin, and of righteousness, and of judgment. v9 OF sin, because they believe not on me. v10, OF righteousness, because I go to my father, and ye see me no more. vll, OF judgment, because the prince of this world is judged. v12, I Have yet many things to say unto you, but ye cannot bear them now. v13, Howbeit when he, the spirit of truth, is come, he will guide you into all truth, for he shall not speak of himself, but whatsoever he shall hear, that shall he speak; and he will shew you things to come. v14, He shall glorify me, for he shall receive of mine, and shew it unto you. v15, All things that the father hath are mine; therefore said I, that he shall take of mine, and shall shew it unto you.

Sometimes singular pronouns are used of the whole Godhead of all three members as a unity (Exod 20:v3, Thou shalt have no other Gods before me. ISA 44:v6, Thus saith the Lord" the king of Israel and his redeemer the Lord of hosts; I am the first and I am the last; and beside me there is no God.

v8, fear ye not, neither be afraid, have not I told thee from that time, and have declared it? ye are even my witnesses. IS there a God beside me? yea there is no God; I know not any. CH 45:v5, I am the Lord, and there is none else, there is no God beside me, I girded thee, though thou hast not known me. v2l, Tell me, and bring them near; yea, let them take counsel together: who hath declared this from ancient time? who hath told it from that time? have not I the Lord? and there is no God else beside me: a just God and a saviour, there is none beside me.

ISA 46: v9, Remember the former things of old: for I am God, and there is none else; I am God, and there is none like me. Hos 13:4, Yet I am the Lord thy God from the land of Egypt, and thou shalt know no God but me, for there is no saviour beside me. Just like the whole church as a unit is spoken of as a man and he (Eph 2: 14-15, For he is our peace, who hath made both one, and hath broken down the middle wall of partition between us. v15, Having abolished in-his flesh the enmity, even the law of commandment contained in the ordinances: for to make in himself of twain one new man, so making peace.

❖ ❖ ❖ ❖ ❖ ❖ ❖ ❖ ❖ ❖ ❖ ❖ ❖ ❖ ❖ ❖ ❖

Eph 4:13, Till we all come in the unity of the faith, and of the knowledge of the son of God, unto a perfect man, who the measure of the stature of the fullness of christ: CH 5:25-27, Husbands, love your wives, even as christ loved,the church, and gave himself for it. v26, That he might sanctify and cleansed it with the washing of water by the word. v27, That he might present it to himself all glorious church, not having spot, or wrinkle, or any such thing, but that it should be holy and without blemish.

2 Thess 2: 7-8,For the mystery of iniquity doth already work: only he who now letteth will let, until he be taken out of the way. v8, And then shall that wicked be revealed, whom the Lord shall consume with the spirit of his mouth, and shall destroy with the brightness of his coming.

## GOD'S CHOICE FOR MAN

Eph 1:4, According as he hath chosen us in him before the foundation of the world, that we should be holy and without blame before him in love. This is what God choose before the overthrow of Lucifer's world-that all of the new race of Adam who accept Jesus Christ should be holy and without blame before him in love. It is this plan that is chosen for all believers, not the individual conformity of any one person to that plan.

The final choice is left up to the individual and not God. All are called and chosen to become holy before God in love if they will accept this plan and choice of God, but only those who meet the conditions will be blessed (John 3:16-20, For God so loved" the world, that he gave his only begotten son, that whosoever believeth in him should not perish, but have everlasting life. v17, For God sent not his son into the world to condemn the world:but that the world through him might be saved. v18, He that believeth on him is not condemned: but he that believeth not is condemned already, because he hath not believed in the name of the only begotten son of God.

v19, And this is the condemnation, that light is come into the world, and men loved darkness rather than light, because their deeds are evil. v20, For every one that doeth evil hateth the light, neither cometh to the light, lest his deeds should be reproved.

Mark 16: 15-16, And he said unto them, go ye into all the world, and preach the gospel to every creature. v16, He that believeth and is baptized shall be saved, but he that believeth not shall be damned. 1 Tim 2: 4, Who will have all men to be saved, and to come unto the knowledge of the truth. 2 Peter 3: 9, The Lord is not slack concerning his promise, as some men count slackness, but is long suffering to us ward, not willing that any should perish, but that all should come to repentance. Rev 22:17, And the spirit and the bride say, come, And let him that heareth say, come, And him that is a thirst come, and whosoever will, let him take the water of life freely.

This is the true meaning of election and predestination wherever found in scripture (Rom 8:29,note) that is, the plan is predestined and foreknown, not the individual conformity to the plan.

## THE WALL OF PARTITION IS BROKEN DOWN

*E*ph 2: 14, For he is our peace, who hath made both one, and hath broken down the wall of partition between us. Here it means that Christ had broken the wall or fence that separated Jews and gentiles, A wall of stone about six feet high that separated the court of the Gentiles from the Jews in the temple. For a Gentile to cross this wall it means death to the Gentile.

Jews always endeavored to live by themselves among the Gentiles. they either wanted a river or wall between them and their Gentile neighbors. Wherever they went their own laws, rites, and customs made a separation between them and the Gentiles.

This latter fact is what is reffered to as the middle wall of partition between Jews and Gentiles. Christ abolished the law of

Moses with all of its commandments, ordinances, and rituals, and provided a new covenant entirely for both Jews and Gentiles, making them one on the same level in all things. To emphasize this, the literal veil in the temple was rent from top to bottom, indicating that the way into holiest had been now made available for all men and that the law was at its end and a new covenant is now ratified.

## MAN MUST LEARN TO DO THE RIGHT THING AS FREE MORAL AGENTS

That God must be respected and obeyed in all things (Eph 3:9-11) And that the laws of God are final and just (PS 119:89) ISA 55:11 ' 2 Tim 3:16-17) That sin does not pay (Gal 6: 7-8) That sin will never be excused(Gen 2:17, Ezek 18:4, Rom 6:23) That sin will be forgiven if terms are met (2 Cor 7: v10, 1 John 1:9) That God's form of government is the only right one (ISA 9:6-7, Rev 20:) That a loving and free submission to God is the highest and most noble principle of moral government Matt 22:37, John 3:16, Rev 22:17, Eph 3:10)

That truth Justice and righteousness must prevail, if any society is to be eternally preserved in the universe (Eph 1:4-12,CH 2:7, CH 3:9-11, Rev 11:15-18, 1 Cor 15: 24-28) That consecration to be the highest good for all of God's people Eph i:4-12, Rev 4: 11, CH 5:11-14, Col 1:15-18) That God is merciful and forgiving to those who will be penitent, and who learn obedience through their fall and redemption (ROM 1: 5,16, CH 3:24-26, CH 16:26, Eph 2:4-10, Titus 2:11-14,CH 3: 5-6) That God is the only absolutely just and perfect being, and the only one capable and worthy of unquestionable authority (ISA 57:13, Rev 4:8, CH 6:10, CH 15: 4).

That all the accusations of present rebels against God are not true (Ezek 28:16, Eph 6:16, Rev 12: v10) That God does only those things which are for the best of creation (Matt 7:7-11,Eph 2:7, Rev 4:11) That God should, by virtue of his own being and position of creator, preserver, Governor, and Lordship, and his own history of justice and righteousness in all of his dealings, will be recognized by all as the supreme moral Governor of the universe(I Cor ll:v3, CH 15:24-28, Eph 2:9-11, Col !:15-18,Rev 4:11) That those who rebel will be punished forever as an everlasting monument of God's wrath on sin and as examples of justice to all coming generation in all eternity (ISA 66:22-24, Rev 14:9-11, Matt 25: 41,46, Mark 9:43-48) That all the redeemed and obedient will become eternal heirs of God and kings and priests under him to help administer the affairs of the universe forever (Dan 7:18,27, Ron 8:17,1 Cor 6:2-3, Eph 2:7,CH 3:9-11,2 TIM 2:12, Rev 1:6, CH 5: 10,CH22:4-5).

## A VISION OF THE APOSTLE PAUL

*I*F I should ask you if you have ever seen the apostle Paul at any time, you would ask me what in the world Am I talking about, If the Lord want us to see what Adam and Eve did look like the day He created them, it would be a very small thing for him to do because He have the negatives of every one and can give us a perfect photo copy of any one looking exactly as they were, so please do not make this a mystery more than it should be.

I saw the apostle Paul in a night vision in the month of may 2007. 1 am not sure why the Lord showed me this man but I had a very good look at him, a man who has become one of the greatest preacher of the new testament church. To see this great man face to face if I,may say-so, is truly more than words can say, it is such a privilege, I do not have words to express myself. may be the Lord want me to remember how much this man endured and had overcome, and if he overcome I can overcome also.

I was in this vision seeing myself putting some papers together to travel to a far country, so when I had all my papers stamp, I went to the waiting area. Then I saw a large crowd of people running to a certain area and I saw a man shaking hands with the people so I ask someone that was also in the waiting area what was happening and the person said its the apostle Paul, so I ask with excitement the apostle Paul? and I ran to the scene, but I did not get to shake his hand because the crowd was swelling very fast, but I could see him very clearly from where I was.

## DESCRIPTION OF THE APOSTLE PAUL

*H*istory said that he was a man of a small stature, I saw the man, and I can say he was about 5 feet six inches to 5 feet seven inches tall, and weigh between 155 to 160 lbs max. From what I observed about the man I can say that there are three things that cannot be denied, and they are humility, dedication, and Sincerity, these three things was pouring out of his face. as one looked at him they could see what he is made of. He was very friendly and of a quiet nature, and of a radiant complexion, it was as if light was under his skin.

## THE ACHIEVEMENT AND CHARACTER OF THE APOSTLE PAUL

*I*t is said that Paul's achievements proclaim him as an unexcelled missionary statesman. He labors by planted churches in the strategic centers of Galatia, Asia, Macedonia, and Achaia, while his plans for work at Rome and in Spain reveal his imperial missionary strategy. His foresight led him to select and train strong young workers to carry on the work after him. Paul was the supreme interpreter of the gospel of Jesus Christ, interpreted to the Gentile world through his labors and letters. It was primarily through his agency that the worldwide destiny of Christianity was established, liberated from the yolk of legalism. His many epistolary writings, formulating, interpreting, and applying the essence of Christianity, are vital to Christian theology and practice. His theology was rooted in his own revolutionary experience with Jesus Christ. He saw man's inability to achieve righteousness through his own efforts, but realized that God had provided a way of salvation, completely out of grace and love in Jesus Christ, available through faith in Christ alone. He also saw that the gospel made strenuous ethical demands upon the life and conduct of the believer.

The essence of the Christian for Paul was union with Jesus Christ, Paul loved and served the Lord Jesus Christ and yearned for his imminent return physically, Paul did not present an imposing appearance, as can be seen from 2 Cor 10:v10, Tradition pictures him as being small of stature, having a decidedly Jewish physiognomy and that he possessed a rugged physical constitution seems clear from all the hardships and sufferings he underwent, as well as his ability amid his spiritual anxieties, to earn his own living through manual labor.

He endured more than most men could endure, yea he keenly felt his bodily frailty. Especially when he was afflicted by a thorn in the flesh. The exact nature of the affliction can only be conjectured; attempts at identifying what it was varied widely. Whatever its precise nature, his feelings of weakness made him constantly dependent upon divine empowerment. The many-sided personality of the apostle Paul is difficult to gather into one picture. He seems to embody polar extremes; bodily weakness and tremendous power, a keen intellect and profound mysticism, strongly attracting and furiously repelling men. Intellectually he was a man of outstanding ability, he was one of the world's great thinkers.

He grasped truth at its full value and logically worked out its implications. But his keen intellect was combined with practical good sense. He was a man of strict integrity, ever careful to maintain a good conscience. His life was characterized by a love of the truth which allowed no time for negotiation for the sake of expediency. Having understood his duty, he followed it unflinchingly, unfettered by possible consequences to himself. He was characterized by native zeal and passion, giving himself wholly to his work.

He was warm-hearted and affectionate, longing for and making strong friendships. He was humble, sincere and sympa-

❖ ❖ ❖ ❖ ❖ ❖ ❖ ❖ ❖ ❖ ❖ ❖ ❖ ❖ ❖ ❖

thetic. HE was by nature a religious man, and his religion, even as a Jew, much more as a Christian, dominated his life activities. The secret of his unique career lay in his fervent nature as possessed and empowered by the living Christ.

## HOW TO GET THE POWER OF GOD

*M*en will have to thirst, drink, and believe to get the baptism of the Holy Spirit: In the last day, that great day of the feast Jesus stood and cried, saying, if any man thirst, let him come unto me and drink. He that believeth on me, as the scripture hath said, out of his belly shall flow rivers of living waters. But this spake he of the spirit which they that believe on him should receive: for the Holy Ghost was not yet given; because Jesus was not yet glorified. (John 7:37-39). This could refer only to the fullness of the baptism of the Holy Spirit received on the day of pentecost, because in Acts 2:33, we read of Jesus being glorified then the Holy Spirit was given to the church. up to this point men had received the spirit in a measure.

Men must hunger and thirst after righteousness to be filled (Matt 5:6) It is clear that the enduement of power is for people who are already children of God. It is not for sinners (JOHN 14:17). The baptism of the Holy Ghost is for people who are already born again and living a holy life for Christ, so please do not called the new birth the baptism of the Holy Ghost, one must hunger and thirst for the things of God and ask God for the baptism of the Holy Spirit.

## HOW TO DO THE WORK OF GOD WISELY

*T*he Christian must learn that he always remain a free moral agent and he can help or hinder the work of God in various ways. Certainly no one would knowingly want to hinder the work of God, but many times people do things ignorantly and yet in all sincerity. The study of the Bible is one of the best ways to help God's work.

Then a person will know what to do under all circumstances. So that one will not have to be doing the wrong things when one acts. One should use any and every measure of the spirit of God that one receives to the glory of God. One may ask what is the work of God? Jesus answered this question when he said, This is the work of God, that ye believe on him whom he hath sent (John 6:28-29).

To believe on the Lord Jesus Christ as the scripture hath said is the greatest work of God men can do. Jesus said if a person would do and do it right he would have rivers of living water flowing out of his innermost being, and he would be able to do greater works than what he had done (John 7:37-39, CH 14:12-15)

## JESUS SAID, MEN SHOULD ALWAYS PRAY AND NOT FAINT

PSALMS 121

David said, I will lift up mine eyes unto the hills, from whence cometh my help. v2 My help cometh from the Lord, which made heaven and earth. v3, He will not suffer thy foot to be moved; he that keepeth thee will not slumber. v4, Behold he that keepeth Israel shall neither slumber nor sleep. v5, The Lord is thy keeper; the Lord is thy shade upon thy right hand. v6, The sun shall not smite thee by day nor the moon by night. v7, The Lord shall preserve thee from all evil: he shall preserve thy soul. v8, The Lord shall preserve thy going out and thy coming in from this time forth, and even for evermore.

PSALMS 124

IF-.it had not been the Lord who was on our side, now may Israel say; v2 IF it had not been the Lord who was on our side, when men rose up against us: v3, Then they had swallowed us up quick, when their warth was kindled against us. v4, Then the waters had overwhelmed us, the stream had gone over our soul. v5 Then the proud waters had gone over our soul. v6, Blessed be the Lord, who hath not given us as a prey to their teeth. v7, Our soul is escaped as a bird out of the snare of the fowlers: the snare is broken, and we are escaped. v8, our help is in the name of the Lord, who made heaven and earth.

PSALMS 125

They that trust in the Lord shall be like mount zion, which cannot be removed, but abideth forever. v2, As the mountains are round about Jerusalem, so the Lord is round about his people from henceforth even for ever. v3, For the rod of the wicked shall not rest upon the lot of the righteous; lest the righteous put forth their hand unto iniquity. v4, Do good, O Lord, unto those that be good, and to them that are upright in their' hearts. v5, As for such as turn aside unto their crocked ways, the Lord shall lead them forth with the workers of iniquity; but peace shall be upon Israel.

PSALMS 128

Blessed is every one that feareth the Lord, that walketh in his ways. v2, For thou shalt eat the labour of thine hands: happy shalt thou be, and it shall be well with thee. v3, Thy wife shall be as a fruitful vine by the sides of thine house: thy children like olive plants round about thy table. v4, Behold, that thus shall the man be blessed that feareth the Lord. v5, The Lord shall bless thee out of zion: and thou shalt see the good of Jerusalem all the days of thy life. v6, Yea thou shalt see thy children's children, and peace upon Israel.

PSALMS 100

Make a joyful noise unto the Lord, all ye lands. v2, serve the Lord with gladness: come before his presence with singing. v3, know ye that the Lord he is God: it is he that made us, and not we ourselves; we are his people, and the sheep of his pasture. v4, Enter into his gates with thanksgiving, and into his courts with praise: be thankful and bless his name. v5, For the Lord is good, his mercy is everlasting and his truth endureth to all generations.

## THE HEART OF THE BIBLE IS THE MESSIAH

PREDICTIONS FULFILLED

Many were astonished at such horrible sufferings of the Messiah (ISA 52:14) His visage was marred more than that of any other man, and his form more than the sons of men. IN his childhood He grew up as a tender plant, and as a root out of a dry ground (ISA 53:2) IN his sufferings He had no beauty of form and no external glory to attract men to himself He was despised and rejected of men (53:v3 He was a man of sorrow and fully acquainted with sickness and pain Men hid (of turned) their faces from him in disgust when they saw his agonies He was despised, and we put no value upon his suffering. The sickness and pain he bore during His sufferings was our very own; yet in view of this we regarded him as suffering justly, smitten by divine judgment, and affleced for his own sins (53: 4) He was slain for our transgressions (because we had sinned: He was crushed for our iniquities: the punishment(chastisement) that secured our peace fell upon him: and with his stripes wounds, bruises,) we were healed (53: 5

The Lord laid upon him the iniquity (our guilt, sins) of us all (53:6) He was maltreated and afflicted, yea He would not open his mouth to complain (53:7) He was as silent and submissive in all his sufferings and was as a lamb brought to the slaughter, and as a sheep before the shearers He was taken from (Heb.Otse, oppression, as in PSALM 107:39 and from judgment (justice): and who can describe the wickedness of his generation? (53:8) He was cut off (violently torn away and slain for no fault of his own) from the land of the living He was slain for the transgressions of his people Israel, the covenant people, they were the ones that should have been slain.

He was buried in a grave with felons and criminals (53:9 He was placed in a rich man's tomb and associated with them in his death Although He had done no violent, and no deceit was found in his mouth, it pleased Jehovah to bruise him for the sake of saving others (53:10) He (Jehovah) out him to grief (Heb. chalah) make sick; diseased; weak; afflicted; painful Jehovah made his soul an offering for sin, the Messiah would have many followers as a result of his offerings

He would prolong his days (or live eternally even though he died) The pleasure of the Lord would prosper in his hand He would see the results of His sufferings and be satisfied (53:. vll) By His knowledge God's righteous servant would make many righteous, for He would bear their iniquities (become sin for them that they might be made the righteousness of God in him, 53:11,2 Cor 5:14-21)

Jehovah was to divide him a portion (or class him) among the great (53:12) The Messiah would divide the spoils of the strong He poured out His soul unto death He was numbered with the transgressors He bore the sin of many, and made intercession for the transgressors.

## FACTS OF PROPHECY ABOUT THE MESSIAH

The literal description of the sufferings of Christ should settle all controversy with Jesus; it proves that their ideas about christ are wrong. It is a matter of history that the Jews interpreted the prophecy in connection with the Messiah until they were pressed to apply it to Jesus of Nazareth; then they were compelled to adopt some other interpretation.

Many began to say that they were two Messiahs one a suffering Messiah, and the other a glorious conqueror. It is true that the Old Testament pictures the Messiah as God and man, king and subject, prince commoner, master and servant, priest and sacrifice, rich and poor, exalted and abased, and eternal yet subject to death, yes, but all this refers to one Messiah only-Jesus on Nazareth.

Some claimed that the Messiah came in the person Hezekiah; others, in modern days some claimed that he has been a good while, but He will not show himself because of the sins of the Jews. Any thing seems acceptable with those who wish to do away with the literal fulfillment of prophecy in Jesus Christ. It was written about 780 years before the suffering of Jesus Christ;

this should settle all controversy with infidels. The description is so particular and minute as to life; work, character, and death of Christ that it could not possible be a guesswork or accidental, but the fulfillment of a divine prearranged plan of God.

Some believe it was a forgery, but Jews would never have forged it because the predictions are absolutely contrary to all their prevailing ideas of the Messiah. They were looking for a great and glorious prince, a conqueror; and this was one of their reason for rejecting Christ. He was of obscure origin and led a despised life. Christians would never think to forged such a prophecy; because Jews guarded their own scripture and know sect could have corrupted the passage.

Furthermore, no Jewish writer has ever pretended that it was not a true prophecy by Isaiah or that it has been changed in any way by Christians to suit their program. The fulfillment could not have been the work of an impostor claiming to fulfill the ancient prophecy to promote his designs, for a large portion of the circumstances did not depend upon the one predicted. But grew out of the feelings and purposes of others seeking to frustrate divine plans. It would be impossible for an impostor to create in this life. IN every detail, the exact coincidences, regarding His experiences, work, character, and death as put forth in the prophecy.

No human being or beings, even those that are in league with satanic powers could have shaped the course of events connected with fulfillment of the prophecy. According to the law of compound probability the 36 separate details of notes U,v2 would have one chance in 68,719,476,736 of fulfillment-This passage is quoted in the new testament several times, as if from a well-known prophecy accepted by all Israel (Matt 8:17, That it might be fulfilled which was spoken by E-saias the prophet, saying, Himself took our infirmities, and bare our sicknesses.

John 12:38, That the saying of E-saias the prophet might be fulfilled, which he spake, Lord, who hath believed our report? and to whom hath the arm of the Lord been revealed? Acts 8: 28-35,

Rom 10:16, But they have not all obeyed the gospel. For E-saias saith, Lord, who hath believed our report? 1 Peter 2: 21-25) The prophecy itself proves that it refers to an individual, not a nation or group of people, for singular personal pronouns are used throughout. His visage being marred more than that of other men: His form, His personal work with men; His being called a man, being rejected, despised, smitten, wounded, and His death, His mouth, grave, the offering of His soul for sin, and many other details could only refer to an individual-the Messiah.

## 2 REASONS WHY ALL MEN SHOULD BELIEVE ISA 53:1

The report itself, God has spoken by the mouth of the prophets since the world began (Acts 3:21, Heb 1:1-3,1 Peter 1:10-12) God, Himself began the long list of prophecies of the coming redeemer by promising that the seed of the woman would crush the serpent's head and restore man's dominion (Gen 3:15-16 Abraham and ISAAC spoke of him coming through their seed (Gen 12:1-3, Gen 15:4-6, Gen 17:4-8, 19-21, Gen 21:12, Gen 26:4 Jacob said He would come from Judah Gen 49:10) Moses predicted him as being a prophet like himself (Deut 18:15-19, David referred to him as coming from his seed (2 Sam 7).Isaiah said He would be born of a virgin in Judah of the house of David (ISA 7:14, Therefore the Lord himself shall give you a sign; behold a virgin shall conceive and bear a son, and shall call his name immanuel.

ISA 9: 6-7. For unto us a child is born, unto us a son is given: and the government shall be upon his shoulder: and his name shalled wonderful counselor, The mighty God, The everlasting faster, The prince of peace. v7, of the increase of his government and peace there shall be no end, upon the throne of David, and upon his kingdom, to order it, and to establish it with judgment and with justice from henceforth even for ever. The zeal of the Lord of hosts will perform this. They pictured His rejection and suffering (CH 52:13 CH 53: 12). others also made reports of his coming, so Israel had no excuse for their unbelief because everything fulfilled according to the words of their own prophets

## MIRACLES CONFIRMING THAT JESUS WAS THE TRUE MESSIAH

*T*he report was not only predicted and then literally fulfilled in Jesus of Nazareth, but there were miracles also confirming to Israel the facts that Jesus was the the true Messiah sent by God (ISA ll:v1-2, And there shall come forth a rod out of the stem of Jesse, and a branch shall grow out of his roots: v2, And the spirit of the Lord shall rest upon him, the spirit of wisdom and understanding, the spirit of counsel and might the spirit of knowledge and the fear of the Lord. CH 42:1-6, Behold my servant, whom I up hold mine elect in whom my soul delighteth; I have put my spirit upon him: he shall bring forth Judgment to the Gentiles.

v2 He shall not cry, nor lift up, nor cause his voice to be heard in the street. v3, A bruised reed shall he not break, and the smoking flax shall he not quench: He shall bring forth judgment unto truth. v4, He shall not fail nor be discourage till he have set judgment in the earth: and the isles shall wait for his law. v5, Thus saith God the Lord, he that created the heavens, and stretched them out: he that spread forth the earth, and that which cometh out of it: he that giveth breath unto the people upon it, and spirit to them that walk therein. v6, I the Lord have called thee in righteousness, and will hold thine hand, and will keep thee, and give thee for a covenant of the people, for a light of the Gentiles.

ISA 61: 1-2, The spirit of the Lord God is upon me; because the Lord hath anointed me to preach good tidings unto the meek; he hath sent me to bind up the broken hearted, to proclaim liberty to the captives and the opening of the prison to them that are bound; v2, To proclaim the acceptable year of the Lord.

Matt 11:1-6, And it came to pass, when Jesus had made an end of commanding his twelve disciples, he departed thence to teach and preach in their cities. v2, Now when John had heard

❖ ❖ ❖ ❖ ❖ ❖ ❖ ❖ ❖ ❖ ❖ ❖ ❖ ❖ ❖ ❖ ❖

in prison the works of christ, he sent two of his disciples v3, And said unto him, art thou he that should come or do we look for another? v4, Jesus answered and said unto them, go and shew John again those things which ye do hear and see. v5, The blind receive their sight, and the lame walk the lepers are cleansed, and the deaf hear, the dead are raised up, and the poor have the gospel preach to them. v6, And blessed is he, whosoever shall not be offended in me.

Luke 4:16-18, And he came to nazareth, where he had been brought up and, as his custom was, he went into the synagogue on the sabbath day, and stood up for to read. v17, And there was delivered unto him the book of the prophet E-saias. And when he had opened the book, he found the place where it was written.

v18, The spirit of the Lord is upon me, because he hath anointed me to preach the gospel to the poor; he hath sent me to heal the brokenhearted, to preach deliverance to the captives, and recovering of the sight to the blind, to set at liberity them that are bruised. (Acts 2: 22, Jesus approved of God) Ye men of Israel, hear these words;-Jesus of Nazareth, a man approved of God among you by miracles and wonders and signs, which God did by him in the midst of you, as ye yourselves also know: Acts 10:38, How God anointed Jesus of Nazareth with the Holy Ghost and with power;who went about doing good, and healing all that were oppressed of the devil; for God was with him.

The arm of the Lord is figurative of his power, Isaiah the prophet predicted would be revealed along with the report (John 5:20, For the father loveth the son, and showeth him all things that himself doeth: and he will shew him greater works than these, that ye may marvel. v36, But I have greater witness than that of John: for the works which the father hath given me to finish, the same works that I do, bear witness of me, that the father hath sent me. John 10:25-38, CH 12:38-4O CH 14:10-12, CH 15:24. NO one will have any excuse for not believing in the Lord Jesus Christ he is our only hope in escaping the judgment of God. Thou ought inexcusable o man whosoever thou art. Neither is there salvation in any other, for there is none other name under heaven given among men, whereby we must be saved Acts 4:12).

Heb 2:1-4, Therefore we ought to give the more earnest heed to the things which we have heard lest at any time we should let them slip. v2, For if the word spoken by angels was steadfast, and every transgression and disobedience received a just recompence of reward: v3, How shall we escape, if we neglect so great salvation: which at first began to be spoken by the Lord, and was confirmed unto us by them that heard him; v4, God also bearing them witness, both with signs and wonders, and with divers miracles, and gifts of the Holy Ghost, according to his own will.

IF they who had the lesser privileges were punished for every sin, what about us who have the greater light in Jesus Christ, we will be punished just the same for every sin. It is a fool's dream to think that there is no moral responsibility on Christians to live right under grace or that grace, does not see their sins if they commit any. Not only was the gospel confirmed then, but it should also be confirmed today by gospel preachers.

### THE GREAT COMMISSION

Mark 16:15-20, And Jesus said unto them, Go ye into all the world, and preach the gospel to every creature. v16, He that believeth and is baptized shall be saved: but he that believeth not shall be damned. v17, And these signs shall follow them that believe, In my name shall they cast out devils: they shall speak with new tongues. v18, They shall take up serpents, and if they drink any deadly thing, it shall not hurt them; they shall lay shall lay hands on the sick and they shall recover. v19, So then after the Lord had spoken unto them, he was received up into heaven, and sat on the right hand of God. v20, And they went forth, and preached every where, the Lord working working with them, and confirming the word with signs following. A-Men.

When Jesus gave his life on the cross, satan believe this was the end of the son of God. But when he rose again on the third day just as he said, the courts of heaven cancelled all the claims of satan, his rights and sovereignty over his victims. He now hold a false authority over them because his head is crushed. His chief method now is intimidation. All who assert their legal, redemptive, blood bought, and divine rights and resist the devil can be free from sin, sickness, and satanic powers. Today all believers in Christ are representatives and officers of God's law and can force the devil to give up strong holds he had on people lives, believers have the power to cast out demons, believers have the power of attorney to act in Christ place here on earth(Mark 16:17-18, John 14:12-15, CH 15:16).

All who refuse to accept what Christ did for them and submit to satan through unbelief are out of the divine will of God and will suffer what they permit satanic forces to do to them (Eph,4:27, CH 6:10-18,). Matt 17:19-20, Then came the disciples to Jesus apart, and said, why could we not cast him out? And Jesus said unto them, Because of your unbelief: for verily I say unto you, If ye have faith as a grain of mustard seed, ye shall say unto this mountain, remove hence to yonder place; and it shall remove, and nothing shall be impossible unto you.

## THE REVELATION OF THE BIBLE

The Bible proves that its Revelation and inspiration is of God. All scripture is given by inspiration of God, and is profitable for doctrine, for reproof, for correction, for instruction in righteousness: That the man of God may be perfect, thoroughly furnished unto all good works (2 Tim 3:16-17).

Knowing this first, that no prophecy of the scripture is of any private interpretation. For the prophecy came not in old time by the will of man: but holy men of God spake as they were moved by the Holy Ghost (2 Peter 1:20-21) This is the first principle of truth, that no prophecy is self originated by the speaker or from a mere impulse of the prophet's own mind. The prophets were borne along or moved by the Holy Ghost. They uttered things far beyond their knowledge and searched diligently for the meaning (1 Peter 1:10-12).

The following reasons are sufficient to prove to an unbiased mind that the Holy Bible is an inspired revelation of God: Take a look at the wonderful unity of the Bible.

Over forty different authors wrote the sixty six books of the Bible during a period of over 1,800 years: and they all had one theme-the creation and redemption of the human race by God through Jesus Christ and the Holy Spirit. These books of the Holy Bible were written by men from all walks such as kings, priests, judges, Lawyers, princes, shepherds, soldiers, courtiers, statesmen, musicians, inventors, singers, poets, preachers, prophets, fishermen, farmers, tent-makers, publicans, physicians, rich man and poor men.

They were written in various lands of three continents-Europe, Asia, and Africa. They were written in different ages and by many men, some who never saw each other or knew what the others wrote on the same subject, yet when their writings became one book, there is not one contradiction among them, this must be God.

IF one should ask forty medical doctors, each from different land and age, they were ask to write forty books on how to cure a disease, what kind of cure would these collection of books present? How much unity would one find among these writers? Collect all forty books of man any subject and one sure to find many contradictions and controversies among these authors. Some would certainly be found trying to prove how wrong the others are and why his theory is right. This is all too apparent to those who have read different authors on any one subject. One would find that there is no unity of thought between the books of man on the same subject.

But there is a perfect unity between the books of the Bible, which speaks of hundreds of subjects in the realm of religion, politics, science, etc, This proves that there is one divine author for all sixty six books. The only author that is capable of producing such a master piece can only be the God and father of our Lord Jesus Christ.

## THE BIBLE IS SUPERIOR TO ALL OTHER BOOKS

There is an abundance of evidence that the Bible is superior to all other books. It is not like any other book in its claims, or in its messages, or in its moral tone, or in its insight into the future, and in its words of peace and comfort and hope to all men in a sinful and dying world. It is different because of its insight into human nature and into all things of life here and the world to come.

It is an outstanding book among millions of books. The Holy Bible is in a class by itself, in its predictions of the future that come's to pass hundreds and thousands of years after its predictions, there is no comparison. The Bible is God's word pleading with the human race that man should not serve satan and sin because the reward is eternal death. There are other books that can be classified as to their subject matter, message, and style, but not so with the Bible. IT does not fit into any human classification of books. Its unique origin, its wonderful structure all prove of its superiority over all other books.

There is also no comparison in its benefits to men, in its circulation, and in its popularity. IN spite of all the competition and the advantage of advertising that other books have over the Bible, it is still the best seller, every year millions of copies are distributed. Millions of men and women all-over the world claimed that the Bible is the only book that satisfies the soul, and gives any hope of life beyond the grave.

When a writer of regular books have his writings translated into a few languages, the author as proud as he can ever be. The Bible has been translated into over a 1000 languages and dialects, and new translations are being made every year. There are many editions of the Bible are made for the blind. It is the most modern book of all ages, all other books are hopelessly outclassed when compared to the Bible. From the standpoint of literature and truth, the Bible is a recognized authority on the affairs of daily life as well as of things in the next life. There is no equal to the Bible. Millions of men and women in all ages have lived and died by its teachings. No such confidence can be placed in any other book. Religions, secret orders, and practically every kind of human doctrine claim to be based upon the Bible, yet there is no comparison.

The Bible is a very simple book to read and understand and yet it needs constant study even unbelievers feels that they are uneducated without a knowledge of the teaching of the Bible.

The more one reads the Bible, the more he realizes he is far short of mastering its contents. There are always new discoveries of truth in the Bible. It is always new to those who read it most. This is not so with other books, because they do not have what it takes to satisfies the soul. When they are read one or two times, there contents are mastered, and the subject matter is no longer interesting. All this proves that the Bible is of a divine origin.

## THE BIBLE HAVE MORE INFLUENCE IN THE WORLD THAN ANY OTHER BOOK

$\mathcal{I}$t is very clear that no other book has influence on the world like the Bible. It has been and still as high as the heaven above the earth in comparison with other books. IN places where the Bible is unknown, this fact can clearly be seen. The Bible is the foundation of many civilization, IN these last days some are rejecting the Bible, the very foundation on which they are built, if the foundation in destroy, such civilization- could be destroyed. It is amazing what pride can do, when they were little and weak they need someone to hold their hand and lead them, God did that for them, but now they are grown big and fat to lofty heights, instead of giving thanks they reject the very God who made them what they are.

Ladies and gentlemen there is a price to be payed for this, such behavior will invite the warth God on their heads, God is not mocked and cannot be mocked, whatsoever a man sow that he will also reap. without the Holy Bible men would be in dense spiritual darkness, and in mental ignorance, believing in pagan superstitution millions of lives has been enlightened and changed in every generation by the teaching of the Bible, this proves that its superior influence must be of divine origin.

## THE BIBLE BUILD CHARACTER

*I*F a person want to know who they really are and who they can be, read the Bible. those who grow in holiness and consecration to the highest good of others, accept the Bible as from God and cherish it more and more and conclude that the Bible is the inspired word of God. Only infidels, skeptics, rebels, and human wrecks of all kinds are the ones who refuse to accept the Bible as the inspired word of God.

Man reject the teaching of the Bible because it condemns all their activities, and promises punishment in the end. The greatest error that ever made is to reject the word of God, believing that their evil ways are right and the divine message of the Bible is wrong, this is a great error.

## DID YOU KNOW

*D*id you know that the Bible tell us the exact day and month Abraham left UR of the Chaldees? This was on the 15th of Nisan or April, exactly 430 years to the day before the children of Israel left Egypt: Now the sojourning of the children of Israel, who dwelt in Egypt, was 430 years. And it came to pass at the end of the 430 years, even the selfsame day it came to pass, that all the hosts of the Lord went out from the land of Egypt Exod 12:40-41). Abraham started the sojourn 430 years to the day before Israel left Egypt, according to this passage. (see also Gen 12:1-3).

Did you know that men travelled through the air many centuries before aircraft start flying? Ezekiel the prophet and philip were both taken through the air by the Holy Spirit (Ezek 8:3, Acts 8:39). John and Paul were taken to heaven and came back (2 Cor 12:1-7, Rev 4:1) Enoch and Elijah were taken to heaven bodily and will come back and die at the hands of the Antichrist Gen 5:24, 2 Kings 2, Heb 11:5, Rev 11: 1-11, Zech 4:11-14). Elijah came back in the day of christ so he had at least two trips to heaven, for he is there now.

Did you know that Me-thu-se-lah was nine hundred and sixty nine years old when he died? Gen 5:27,

Did you know that Saul was not the first king of Israel, the truth is that Israel had a king over 500 years before Samuel the prophet made Saul king? Moses was Israel first king according to (Deut 33:4-5)

Did you know that God did not create sin and that he is not responsible for it? sin is the transgression of the law of God. 1 John 3:4, Whosoever committeth sin transgresseth also the law: for sin is the transgression of the law. God created creatures capable of laws and He made laws, but He did not make them break the law. Those who break the law are responsible and God hold them responsible for their behavior.

Did you know that the hinderer of lawlessness in 2 Thess 2:7-8 refers to the church? There are only three things in the world today that hinder lawlessness. And they are the church, the Holy Spirit, and human governments. The hinderer that will be taken out of the world must refer to one of these three things. It could not refer to the Holy Spirit and human government for neither will be taken out of the world. It is clear that governments will not be taken out because Antichrist will reign over ten kingdoms during the tribulation (Dan 7:23-24, Rev 17:8-17) The Holy Spirit will be here during the tribulation, so He could not be the hinderer that will-be taken out (Acts 2:16-21, John 14:16; Rev 7:14, CH 12:17, CH

19:10; Zech 12:10)

The church will be taken out of the world 1 Thess 4:16, Eph 5:26-27, 1 Cor 15:51-58) So this must be the hinderer referred to. IF you cannot understand how the church could be referred to as "he" see Eph 2:15, CH 4:13, where the church is called a man.

Did you know that the mark on Cain was not a physical mark or change of color? The Hebrew word for mark in Gen 4:15, means a pledge. The pledge was stated in the same verse Therefore whosoever slayeth Cain, vengeance shall be taken sevenfold.) There is no statement that he was marked physically by a change of color or some other mark.

Did you know that the colored race started after the flood and not with cain? This is clear from the fact that all mankind was destroyed in Noah's flood and all the different races had to start after the flood.

IN Acts 17:26, we are told that of one blood God hath made all nations of men to dwell upon the whole face of the earth. How was this brought about is clear from the fact two nations came from Lot's two daughters (Gen 19) and two other nations came from Rebekah (Gen 25:23). No one knows just when the first colored child was born so all speculations are worthless.

Did you know that there was a man who was healed of leprosy three different times?. This man was Moses, Moses was a sign to Israel and pharaoh three times when his hand made leprous and was healed (Exod 4:6-7,21,30).

Did you know that Isaiah son Mahershalal-hash-baz is not the longest name in the Bible as stated in all Bible statistics of men? There is another name equally as long found in the title of the 56th PSALM, the eighteen letters of Isaiah son mean haste ye, haste ye to the spoil, because Judah was soon to be spoiled by babylon and the Jews taken into captivity, see Isa 8:3).

Did you know that 200,000,000 horsemen will soon appear on the earth to slay millions of men? IN the future tribulation during the six trumpet Judgment when four angels will be loosed that are now bound in river Euphrates, when they are loosed 200,000,000 demon or spirit horsemen will be loosed out of the bottomless pit. Each of these four angels will lead 50,000,000 of these demon horsemen in a different direction to slay one third of all men at a certain hour (Rev 9:13-21) This will literally happen in the first three and one half years of Daniel's seventieth week, for the middle of the week starts with the seventh trumpet (Rev 11:15-18, CH 12:6,14; CH 13:5).All these events will take place after the rapture as proved in Rev 4:1, which says all the events of Rev 4, through Rev 22, must be hereafter, that is after the church is raptured.

Did you know that sinners can commit the unpardonable sin? This is very clear from the fact the Jews of Matt 12:22-37, were sinners and Jesus warned them of committing that sin. IN Heb 10:26-29, we have the fact that a person who has been sanctified by the blood of Jesus Christ can go back into sin and commit this sin.

The blasphemy against the Holy Spirit and attributing to the devil the works of the Holy Spirit, or speak a word against the Holy Spirit knowingly and willfully, is the unpardonable sin, and any person can commit this sin whether he is a sinner or not. A person must be very careful what they say against a person who are being used by the Holy Spirit.

Did you know that there is one man in the Bible who fasted longer than Jesus did? This man was Moses, Moses fasted at least three times forty days each (Deut 9:9-11, 17-18,23-25). IN fact, it seems from Deut 9:11-18, that Moses fasted eighty days without eating between the two forty days fasts.

Did you know that there is one man in the Bible who captured a whole army of multiplied thousands single-handed?. Elisha the prophet did this when he captured the whole army of Syria and led them captive to Samaria (2 Kings 6:18-23).

Did you know that Egypt will never become great again? The Bible is very clear that Egypt will never be a great power again as it used to be in the early days of Israel. The prophet Ezekiel said that Egypt would be a base kingdom. It shall be inferior of the kingdoms. Neither shall it exalt itself any more above the nations"(Ezek 29:14-15). Egypt will be defeated in the future by the Antichrist from Syria (Dan 11:40-45).

Did you know that the Arabs will give Israel protection from the Antichrist during the last three and one-half years of this age? Dan 11:41, States that Arabia or ancient Edom and Moab will escape the ANtichrist. IN Isaiah 16:1-5, Ezek 20:33-35, Matt 24: 15-21, Rev 12:5-17, We read of Israel fleeing for protection into the wilderness of Edom and Moab, and since they escape the Antichrist and flee into this country for protection, then it is clear that the Arabs protect them during this time.

It does not look like it now because many want to get rid of them but that will not happen because the words of the prophets are sure, they will not fall by the side of the road, they will accomplish to that which it is sent.

Did you know that the Bible names the very city in Edom and Moab that Israel will flee to for protection during the tribulation?. The name of the city is Sela or petra, the ancient capital of Edom (Isa 16:1-5,CH 26:20-21, CH 63:1-8).

IN Matt 24:15-16, Jesus said, When ye therefore shall see the abomination of desolation, spoken by Daniel the prophet, stand in the Holy place, who so readeth, let him understand.) Then let them which be in Judea flee into the mountains.(Edom and Moab.) The abomination refers to the Antichrist and his image in the Jewish temple at Jerusalem during the last 3.-2 years of this age.

## WHAT DOES IT MEAN TO DREAM THAT YOU ARE FLYING?

*W*E humans don't fly so why would we dream that we are flying? This does not make sense to the person who don't know the importance of a dream. Flying is good if you are in control of what is taking place. This dream can let you know if things are faverable for you are not, to fly over muddy water is not good, to fly over clear blue water is good,if you are being chased by some one or some thing and get caught, that is bad, you are in trouble, enemy is at your door, dreams are telling us things so we can avoid what is coming. IF you outfly your enemy means you are strong and will overcome what is coming your way.

Flying is my way of getting away from danger, I had this dream many times, more than any other dream, at first I did not understand the meaning of this dream but after having this dream so many times I got a clear understanding of what this dream is saying.

This dream is also a test of faith, so please pay attention to this. If you should dream that you are standing on the top of a twenty story building or some other high place and there is no other way down but to fly, what would you do? you will have to make a decision either to sit there like a chicken or take off like an eagle. I have been tested many times with this dream. God could be testing you and you don't realize that he is doing it, Some times in this dream I have to make a conscious decision within myself, I have to know that I can fly, If I cannot make that decision to fly I would fail the test but thank God I pass this test, and the same goes for you. We don't have wings yet we have to know that we can fly, this is faith, If you cannot do it because you were fearful, your faith is weak, so you need to examine yourself to see whether you are in the faith or not.

IF you can take to the air without hesitation means your faith and confident in the lord is strong. (Attention please) In one one of my flight I take off-from the top of a very high building and I circle around and landed in front of a large crowed of people, and a man came up to me and ask how I did it, so I explain to him that I have to know that I can fly and that is how I was able to do it, that is faith. Faith is more than believing, much more, the devil himself believe and tremble, faith turns the wheel of motion, faith act, faith let you do what seems impossible to others.

ATTENTION PLEASE, What I am telling you here is not

✧ ✧ ✧ ✧ ✧ ✧ ✧ ✧ ✧ ✧ ✧ ✧ ✧ ✧ ✧ ✧ ✧

my idea or what I think, it is the revelation of the Lord. When we are in a dream the Lord is dealing with our spirit which is the real you, your body is the house where the real person you lives Your spirit look exactly as you are now no different, I saw them both in a night vision so I do know.

Some dreams teach us also how to use our faith, what I mean is this, the same confident that give you the victory in your dream use it in your waking life and you will do well. Please listen to this and you will understand what I am saying. I dream one night that I went to a building, the building look like a manufacturing place, there was no light in the building it was in total darkness, the machine in the building that responsible for the lighting of the building was off and my faith rise up in me and I call to the machine and said in the name of Jesus turn on and the machine turn itself on and all the lights came on in the building. It is clear that this is faith, the Lord is saying to me that the same faith that I use to turn the machine on I should use it in real life and I will get the result.

## WHAT DOES IT MEAN TO DREAM OF A LARGE FOREST WITH RANGERS ON IT

One night I dream that I was flying from one point to another, I was on my way home so I choose to take a short cut by flying over this forest that was very large, it was tens of thousands of acreage of land. As I flew over this forest I could see many fruit trees on the property and some wild food growing in the ground, I saw some poor people on the property digging in the ground to get the wild food that grow there. then I saw 4 or 5 rangers running towards those poor people to arrest them, and the people was afraid, and started to ran in panic, and they were saying we are going to go to jail, and I became very sorry for the people, and decide to take on the rangers so that the people could escape. These rangers had machete and two swords was given to me and I attack them, with one sword in my right hand and the other sword in my left hand.

The fight was long and vicious, they fight to kill, they were strong and dangerous they have muscles like weight lifters but I prevailed. These rangers were like people but they were not people, I run my sword through them but they did not bleed and they could not die. I prevailed over them because greater is he that is in us than he that is in the world.

This is the interpretation of the dream, The large forest is the world, those heartless rangers are demonic forces that work for the devil, those poor people are the sinners of the world, without christ they are poor, naked, and blind, so they need our help to deliver them from the power of satan. Take the sword of the spirit which is the word of God, they need our help.

## KNOW THE WORD OF GOD

$\mathcal{A}$ person must be thoroughly familiar with the word of God because faith cometh by hearing, and hearing by the word of God" (Rom:10:17,To him give all the prophets witness, that through his name whoever believeth in him shall receive remission of sins. While Peter yet spake these words, the Holy Ghost fell on all them which heard the word, Acts 10:43-44, 1 Cor 1:18-2.4;, Says, For the preaching of the cross is to them that perish foolishness: but unto us which are saved it is the power of God. v19, For it is written, I will destroy the wisdom of the wise, and will bring to nothing the understanding of the prudent. v20,Where is the wise? where is the scribe? where is the disputer of this world? hath not God made foolish the wisdom of this world? v2l For after that in the wisdom of God the world by wisdom knew not God, it pleased God by the foolishness of preaching to save them that believe.

v22, For the Jews require a sign, and the Greeks seek after wisdom: v23, But we preach Christ crucified, unto the Jews a stumbling block, and unto the Greeks foolishness: v24, But unto them which are called, both Jews and Greeks, Christ the power of God, and the wisdom of God. v25, because the foolishness of God is wiser than men: and the weakness of God is stronger than men.

Human eloquence is no substitute for the anointing power of the Holy Spirit, v17, It pleased God to confound the wise of that day by the preaching of the crucified Christ. The Jews would not have him because they excepted the Messiah to come as a mighty conqueror. When he came to be crucified they stumbled at him and would not believe. The Gentiles could not see any reason for salvation by a crucified malefactor of Judea .But to those that believe, Christ was the power and wisdom of God. Gal 3:11,2 Thess 2:13).

After accepting Christ the next thing to do is to start reading the Bible and to meditate on God's word day and night. We are promise in God's word that if a man would do this he would be like a tree that is planted by the rivers of water that will bring forth its fruit in its season and that what soever he doeth shall prosper (PSALM 1, Josh 1).

Too many people are praying and never think of what God's word says concerning what they are asking God for, many people do pray but do not use the word of God in their prayer to go along with what they are praying about.

The word of God and prayer must go together if definite results are to be expected. God honour his word and will do what he says he will do. The Lord is not slack concerning promise, as some men count slackness 2 Peter 3:9. It is the Bible that reveals the will of God in all things concerning his promises when we pray by faith.

## DO YOU HAVE FAITH OR YOU ARE PRAYING FOR IT?

To pray for faith is a prayer of unbelief, that means you do not take God at his word, and there cannot be an answer to that prayer. prayer for faith is simple an attempt to avoid faith in the in the word of God and get things from God contrary to truth.

The word of God alone can give us the basis for answered prayer. Simple faith in the word of God may not be considered sufficient or even sensible to the natural man who lives in his senses and who always want to see and feel every thing with which he has to do, but this kind of confidence is necessary if one wants the promises of God. We are not told to pray for faith, but to have faith in God. IN Mark 11: 22-24, And Jesus answering saith unto them, Have faith in God. v23, For verily I say unto you, That whosoever shall say unto this mountain, Be thou removed, and be thou cast into the sea; and shall not doubt in his heart, but shall believe that those things which he saith shall come to pass, he shall have whatsoever he saith. v24, Therefore I say unto you, What things soever ye desire, when ye pray, believe that ye receive them, and ye shall have them.

## FIND YOURSELF A GOOD CHURCH

It is very important for God's people to listen to good preaching, preachers who are filled with the anointing power of the Holy Ghost on their lives, without the anointing they keep the church cold and dead like themselves, we only have one Holy Ghost, we either filled with his anointing power or we don't. The baptism of the Holy Spirit does not keep us cold, and dry and dead, He give us power to do the work of Christ.

IN John 7:37-39, It is written, IN the last day, that great day of the feast, Jesus stood and cried, saying, if any man thirst, let him come unto me and drink. v38, He that believeth on me, as the scripture hath said out of his belly shall flow rivers of living water. v39, But this spake he of the spirit, which they that believe on him should receive, for the Holy Ghost was not yet given, because that Jesus was not yet glorified.

Any church that-let you feel like you are sitting in an elementary school room, find some where else to worship God.

Never let any one use their fancy speech of eloquence to keep you trap in a cold dead church, your soul salvation worth far more than a beautiful church building, your soul salvation worth far more than rubies, silver, diamond or gold preachers have an obligation and that is to feed the flock. IN Acts 20:28, We read, Take heed therefore unto yourselves, and unto all the flock over which the Holy Ghost hath made you overseers to feed the church of God, which he hath purchased with his own blood. After a sunday morning service we should be able to say, it is good for us to be here.

Church should be a place where people go to see the power of God on display flowing from the pulpit to the pews. Good preaching inspires and set-the soul on fire, good preaching lift burdens and set the captives free, good preaching break the yoke and set your spirit free. Many people have problems of all kinds, so when they go to church they are hoping to hear a message from God to help lift the burden, but instead, all they get is a long boring sermon that did nothing for them, so they went home the way they came, God's people deserve better than that.

Talking scripture are very different from preaching the gospel with the anointing power of the Holy Ghost. When we hear constantly the stories of the triumphs of people of faith in the Bible, when we read of miracles such as how dividing the red sea, and the river Jordan, how God rain manna from heaven and sending quails, or birds, how He give Israel water from rocks, how God multiplied food, when we hear of the raising of the dead, and the healing of the sick, and how men through faith they quenched the violence of fire, how they escaped the edge of the sword, out of weakness they were made strong, waxed valiant, or strong in fight, how they turned to flight the armies of the aliens, and many many more of other miraculous events that are written in scripture for our instruction and up our faith in the Lord, our faith will run high, knowing that what God had done then, He can do it again when we meet His obligations and will give us what He has promised.

(REMEMBER) It is very important for Christians to remember their past experiences with the Lord, they help one to strive to get back to where they once were in the Lord, the Bible said we are to remember, Rev 2:5, Remember therefore from whence thou art fallen, and repent, and do the first works; or else I will come unto thee quickly, and will remove thy candlestick out of his place, except thou repent.

What many pulpit need today is the anointing power of the Holy Ghost, it is badly needed. The anointing will lift burdens and break the yoke, talking scripture do not lift burdens and break yoke, the anointing break the yoke.

Church leaders call for a week of revival services and after a week of services condition remain the same, church leaders need to understand that talking scripture do not bring about revival, revival is a spiritual awakening or renewal, whether to the saving of souls or reviving of the saints, this can only come about through the anointing power of the Holy Ghost.

Jesus said, The spirit of the Lord is upon me, because he hath anointed me to preach the gospel to the poor; he hath sent me to heal the brokenhearted, to preach deliverance to the captives, and recovering of sight to the blind, to set at liberty them that are bruised, Luke 4:18).

IF Jesus need the anointing power of the Holy Ghost to do the work of the father, what about us? Paul said, And I, brethren, when I came to you, came not with excellency of speech or of wisdom, declaring unto you the testimony of God. For I determined not to know any thing among you, save Jesus Christ, and him crucified. And I was with you in weakness, and in fear, and much trembling. And my speech and my preaching was not with enticing words of man's wisdom, but in demonstration of the spirit and of power: That your faith should not stand in the wisdom of men, but in the power of God,(1 Cor 2:1-5).

Paul was determined not to introduce any other knowledge,

❖ ❖ ❖ ❖ ❖ ❖ ❖ ❖ ❖ ❖ ❖ ❖ ❖ ❖ ❖ ❖ ❖

or esteem any other doctrine worthy of notice, save Jesus Christ and the benefits of the cross, Paul speak of his weakness which could be physical, or an expression of utter dependence on God. IF physical, it was no doubt the result of Paul's stoning, beating, and other sufferings of 2 Cor 11:24-27, Gal 4:13. The fear and trembling Paul talked about could be a state of mind, dreading lest he should grieve the Lord and bring reproach upon the truth (1 Cor 9:27,2 Cor 7:15, Eph 6: v5,) Paul stand firmly against using any persuasive doctrine of human wisdom. I used none of the means of a great and skilled speaker to sway men, I Preach under the anointing and power of the spirit and confirmed what I preach with signs following (Rom 15:18-19,29, Acts 19-:11) I used this method so that your faith might be in the power of God, and not in human wisdom v 4-6)

The wisdom of God is in the gospel of Jesus Christ, which was hidden up to the time of its revelation and which God ordained before this age for us. None of the rulers of the world knew about this revelation. IF they had known any thing about this revelation they would not have crucified the Lord Jesus Christ-prophets searched diligently to understand what they prophesied about it, and even angels themselves desired to comprehend it (1 Peter 1:10-13) such mystery is now made clear through the preaching of the apostles and the revelation of the scripture of the N.T.(Rom 1:1-5, CH 16:25-26; 1 Cor 2:9-16, Gal 1:12,16; Eph 3:1-8;Heb 8:6; 2 Peter 3:16

## LISTEN YOUNG LOVERS

*T*he Lord can let you know when things are not working out for you if you ask him to guide you, this is a true dream I have seen the result of it, so please pay attention. . IF you are in love with a young lady and one night you dream that she pack your clothes in a bag, and came and drop it at your feet, walk away it is over, it is time to go she is not in love with you.

Marriage is based on love and not trust, if that trust is broken you have nothing left, but if you marry for love, love suffereth long, it is just amazing what love can handle. Why would you want others to trust you when you cant even trust yourself, why? Those who do not believe in dreams is like a man walking with his eyes closed, he is not aware of what is before him. The prophet Micah said, Trust ye not in a friend, put ye not confidence in a guide: keep the doors of thy mouth from her that lieth in thy bosom, Micah 7:v5)

## ARE YOU HINDERING THE HOLY SPIRIT FROM WORKING?

*M*any believers are hindering the working of the Holy Spirit because of the way they live, Paul said, And grieve not the Holy Spirit of God, whereby ye are sealed unto the day of redemption, Eph 4:30. He is a person and can be grieved. Paul said, Quench not the spirit, He can be turned off, so it is very important for Christians to live a life of holiness so that the Holy Spirit can work through us freely.

Many religious leaders also are hindering the working of the Holy Spirit with their religious rules and do not understand that they are doing it, their religious rules are more important than what the Holy Spirit have to say to the church. The Holy Spirit can only work through believers to deliver a message, unless they want God to raise up stones to deliver that message, God's people are not free in many churches because if you rejoice and shout in these church they will put you out or they will tell you to keep quiet.

Lets talk about speaking with unknown tongue. Some leaders do not want tongues in their-church because they do not understand what the person is saying, so they use 1 Cor 14:28, which says, But if there be no interpreter, let him keep silence in the church, and let him speak to himself, and to God. They ignore v39-40, Wherefore, brethren covet to prophesy, and forbid not to speak with tongues let all things be done decently and in order.

The Bible did not tell us to cut tongues out of the church. It is better to pray and ask the Lord for an interpreter, l have seen it happen how God raised up interpreter where there was no interpreter, so that the church could understand what the holy Spirit was saying through the believer. When tongues are totally silence in the church, it is not only the believer that will be silence but also the message that could come from those believer will be also silence. God hear and answer prayer so lets pray.

Listen to this, What I am about to tell you happen in the late 1950's in Jamaica- A few ladies started a new church and after a few years they were still all ladies, no men was in the church so they started to pray asking God to give them a man to lead them and the Lord answer the prayer of those ladies. The Lord save a young man from the district and talk to him in a dream to go to that church. When the young told the church the story they know the Lord had answered their prayer and he became the pastor of that church. He was highly anointed, they called him the second Paul. I have been to that church and his brother who was now a member of the church told me the story. God hears and answer prayer. Confess your faults one to another, and pray one for another, that ye may be healed. The effectual fervent prayer of a righteous man availeth much, James 5:16).

## GOD PROMISE TO ANSWER PRAYER

*I*F I shut up the heaven that there be no rain, or if command the locust to devour the land, or if I send pestilence among the people. IF my people, which are called by my name, shall humble themselves, and pray, and seek my face, and turn from their wicked ways; then will I hear from heaven, and will forgive their sin, and will heal their land. 2 Chron 7:13-14. When people repent and pray God will hear and command the clouds to send rain, and command the locust to leave the land, and command pestilence to leave his people. God is a kind, loving, and merciful

God who will honour his word, He will do what He said he will do. God will reverse any judgment if His people would pray and seek His face.

I heard these words in a night vision, which says the Lord will do what he said He will do, they were not my thoughts, I heard it.

## THE IMPORTANCE OF REPENTANCE

*G*od talk to the prophet Jonah to go to Nine-veh which was a great city with 120,000 inhabitants and much cattle. Nine-veh WAS built by Asshur in the days after the flood of Noah (Gen 10:11-12) It was the capital of Assyria, situated on the river Tigris, and was first called Nina, from the patron goddess of the city. IN Jonah 1:v1, We read, Now the word of the Lord came unto Jonah the son of A-mitta-l, saying, v2, arise, go to, go to Nine-veh, that great city and cry against it; for their wickedness is come up before me. IN CHAPTER 3:v4, jonah cried against the city and said, yet forty days, and Nine-veh shall be over-, thrown.

v5, said, So the people of Nine-veh believed God, and pro-claimed a fast, and put on sackcloth, from the greatest of them even to the least of them. The king lay aside his robe covered himself, and sat in ashes (v6) A decree was made by the nobles that no man or beast should eat food or drink water, and that all should be covered in sackcloth, and that every one should cry mightily to GOD (v7-8) It was also decreed that all men should turn from their evil ways and violence (v8). v10, And God saw their works, that they turned from their evil ways, and God repented of the evil, that he had said that he would do unto them, and he did it not. It is clear that God will change his mind from any judgment if people would repent.

Jesus denounces the Jews because they would not repent Luke (11:31, Matt 11:20) and approved the story of Jonah. IN Matt 12:41, Jesus said, The men of Nine-veh shall rise in Judgment with this generation, and shall condemn it; because they repented at the preaching of Jona's; and behold, a greater than Jonas is here.

## A VISION OF A SERPENT THAT KILLED A PREACHER

*O*ne night I had a dream about a preacher and myself, we both was standing on the side of a hill and there came a very heavy shower of rain and all the water from off the hill created a pond in the valley below, so the preacher was washed away by the water down into the valley for reasons I do not know. So I ran down to the valley to help him out of the water, but he was already grabbed by a very large serpent, and the serpent wrapped him. This was a very strong man and he fought with all his might to get away from the serpent, but the power of the serpent was too much for him. When he realize he could not get away, I heard him said ok, ok, and he gave up to the serpent, and the serpent crushed him.

When you read about this vision it may not seem much to you but this was a very, very, terrifying dream I was there and heard his groaning when the serpent was crushing him, so he died. This preacher was sick but I did not know at the time when I had the dream, he died about one year after this dream.

This is the interpretation of the dream, The heavy shower of rain that wash away the preacher, means that his illness would take him to the valley of death and there he would die. Death is an enemy so the serpent represent this enemy, death, the serpent took his life. So until Jesus comes we must all prepare to face this enemy, death.

## THE POWER OF DREAMS

*I*t is just amazing what a dream can do, when the gospel cannot reach some people the Lord may use a dream, I have a niece who can testify to this fact how the Lord talk to her in a dream, and there are thousands of people all over the world that can say the same. I listened to a Moslem man who speaks of how he was not satisfied with his moslem religion but he did not know what to do, and the Lord spoke to him in a dream and told him to change his way of thinking, so he become a Christian. And many, many more from moslem religion are coming to christ because of a dream. If one person accept christ because of a dream, it would be enough for me to pray this prayer, Lord please give us more dreams.

For a moslem to leave their religion and to embrace Christianity, this is done in the face of great danger because they could be hunted down like a wild dog and be killed, so let us pray for them that God will keep them safe. This is the kind of religion they belong to, this is certainly not God, this is the devil at his best. The moslem people need to understand that God made man a free moral agent, that they are free to choose between Mohammed and Jesus christ, moslems need to understand that Mohammed cannot save them, Mohammed did not gave his life on the cross to washed away their sins, Jesus Christ the son of God did that. Mohammed cannot forgive your sins, Jesus will, that's why he died, Mohammed cannot heal you when you are sick, Jesus will.

Peter defend himself after a man who was born lame from birth that by the power of Jesus name the man was made whole. Then Peter, filled with the Holy Ghost, said unto them, ye rulers of the people, and elders of Israel. IF we this day be examined of a good deed done to the impotent man, by what means is he made whole. Be it known it unto you all, and to all the people of Israel, that by the name of Jesus Christ of Naz-a-reth, whom ye cruci-fied, whom God raised up from the dead, even by him doth this man stand here before you whole. This is the stone which was set at naught of you builders, which is become the head of the corner. Neither is there salvation in any other: for there is none other name under heaven given among men, whereby we must be saved.

Some will say that all religion is good because they are all calling on God and worshipping the same God, this is a big mis-take to believe that because many worship and know not what they worship.

There is a big difference between true worshippers and false worshippers. Jesus said, But the hour cometh, and now is, when the true worshippers shall worship the father in spirit and in truth: for the father seeketh such to worship him. God is a spirit, and they that worship him must worship him in spirit and in truth, John 4:23-24. God is a spirit being, not the sun, moon, stars, nor an image of wood, or metal, God is not a beast or man, God is not the air, wind or universal mind, or some impersonal quality. God is a person with a real spirit body, a personal soul, and spirit like the angels Heb 1:v3. God is a person, just like Jesus is a person, philip said to Jesus shew us the father, Jesus said, you are looking at him, (John 14:8-9).

## DISCERNING OF SPIRITS, HOW DOES THIS GIFT WORK?

It is an ability which the Holy Spirit gives some Christians to discern between those who spoke by the Spirit of God and those who were moved by false spirits. The phrase is found in 1 Cor 12:10, and is one of the gifts of the Spirit. How does this gift work? What I-,am writing to you here is very real. I know a discerner lady many years ago, she was a member of the first church that I pastor. She was walking to church one sunday morning and the Holy Spirit showed her a witchcraft worker about half a mile away coming toward her, this was a very winding road in the country area so she could not see the man, so she started to shout, witchcraft worker, witchcraft worker until they pass each other.

When they met the witchcraft worker said to her, witchcraft worker nu, but she just kept going, she did not turn around to look at him, and the Holy Spirit showed her the man standing in the road behind her looking at her. This was not an imagination, this was real, she did not turn around. This is the gift of discerning in action. This was not a lady for any man to call baby, she was a serious discerner. These gifts are from God and must be used for him. The Holy Spirit reveal a lot of things to discerners, they can see you miles away, a discerner has extraordinary power in detecting evil and what is happening in the church. This lady ask me a question one day, she ask me if I ever read a book entitled future, I told her I never read the book, but the Lord showed me the book in a night vision about two weeks before, I never told any one the vision I had about the book and yet she know about me and the book, I never saw the book in real life, the Lord showed me the book.

Two weeks before I announce to the church that I was leaving she came to church one sunday morning and as she was praying the Holy Spirit showed me to her walking out of the church, meaning, I was leaving and no one know that I was planning to leave. She was a true discerner.

This gift completes the gifts of revelation in the realm of knowledge. Every thing that could be known concerning the past, present, and future of all creations, or what may be known of God and his plans and purposes all comes within the range of three gifts, wisdom, knowledge, discernment. They can make known all that God sees fit to reveal to his servants. This gift is just as miraculous as others, but it operates in the spiritual realm only.

The purpose of this gift is to give an insight into the spirit realm and reveal the kind of spirit that is working in and through a person, and make known thoughts and motives. It conveys information concerning spirits that could never be learned apart from this gift. Discernment of things outside the spirit realm is the work of man's wisdom and knowledge.

## A VISION OF A WHITE JACKET

To dream that you hang your white jacket, dress, or coat and when you return to get it, it was not there, you could not find it, but when you did found it, it was on the floor somewhere else walked on by others, and it was dirty and looking terrible. It mean that your reputation is under attack.

## A COW

*T*o dream that you was attacked by a cow and you grab the beast by the horn and subdue it, that mean you will overcome your enemy, but if it overcome you, you could be defeated if you are not on your guard. when a person have dreams of this kind you must stay alert.

A dog. To dream that you are attacked by a vicious dog and you chase it away from you, victory will be yours, but if bitten you will suffer loss, enemy is working against you.

## A CAT

*C*ats are enemies, if you are bitten or scratched by one you will suffer loss, but if you kill it or chase it away from you, you will over your enemy. The secret is to remember your dream and pay attention.

## A FAMILY MEMBER

*T*o dream of a family member could mean many things, it all depends on the nature of the dream. One night I dream that one of-my brother and myself was traveling on a road, he was a little way back behind me, he was grabbed by an officer looking more like a soldier, he was kicking and screaming so I rush back to help him but the officer was strong and drag him away before I could help him. This brother don't know the Lord. The officer is an agent of satan that work for him.

## A SECOND DREAM

*A*bout 4 or 5 months after the first dream I had a second dream about him, this time he telephone somebody that he was hurt and need help. The person told me and I rush to the place where he call from but I could not find him, then I saw a man and I told him that I was looking for my brother and he told me where he think he was, so I went to the place and called him and he heard me and answer but his voice was very faint or very low, it sound as if he was in a hole in the ground he certainly was not on top where he could be seen, the place was a forest with dense bush; I did not find him but he was there being trapped somewhere.

This dream speaks of the sinful condition that he is in and need help just as he said.

## MY DISTRIBUTOR

One night I dream that I was in a vicious sword fight with my distributor who was buying my tambourine, I did not want to fight with him because in the dream he was my friend, but he leave me with no choice but to fight because I could see that he want to kill me. I woke from the dream, I think about it but could not see any reason why he would want to fight with me. Although I could not see any reason for the fight the dream was telling me that trouble was coming.

Then about thirty days after the first dream I had another dream, this time I went to his place of business in the dream and I saw a man sitting on the floor and he gave the man one of my tambourine and the way the man was looking at it by turning it over and over again examining it I know he was going to make a copy of it and that was exactly what happen. So he ordered some tambourine from me, and when. I deliver his order I told him the dream I had, he said I was going to bed too late and that I dream too much.

About eight or nine months later I went to the head office of a music store to show them a new tambourine that I invented, when the gentleman saw it he said I have some similar to this so he brought one to show me, he said he bought 200 from this distributor which was my distributor I never sold him 200 at any one time so I know something was wrong. I also spoken to the owner of another company who was buying hundreds from him so I know he was getting them from off shore.

I talk to him about the matter several times but he deny it all so I stop doing business with him. Dreams are a great communicator, they are talking to us, they let us know the secret and hidden things, we just have to pay attention. A dream can take you to heaven so you can see what heaven look like, a dream can take you to hell so you can see what hell look like, there is no limit to what God can reveal through dreams.

There are some people that I called Christian unbelievers because they refuse to believe God, they want God to send angels to talk to them in real life for them to believe. My God don't have to send angels to me in real life for me to believe because what the angel is going to tell me in real life he can tell me the same thing in a dream, if the Lord choose to send me an angel in real life then to God be the glory.

## A VISION ABOUT TWO BROTHERS

After I stop doing business with the first company another company started to buy the product from me, then one night I had a dream that I went to an office to show them my new tambourine, and I leave it on a table for about a minute, when I return the tambourine was gone. When I woke from the dream I know somebody stole the tambourine, so I just keep my eyes open. Then not long after that I had a second dream that I was in a large and beautiful building looking more like a plaza that had many stores in it, I was on the second floor walking down the stairs to the first floor, on the stairs were two brothers standing on the stairs with their hands out stretched blocking me so that I could not pass, and they were very serious, I could not pass them, but I was determine to pass so I grab onto an overhead bar and swing myself over their head and that is how I was able to pass them.

These two brothers are the owners of this new company, for a few months they buy the product from me and stop, but they were still selling the product from their catalogue and website and tradeshow, they did the same thing as the first company.

Dreams are true and must be taken seriously. IF my experience and explanation are not good enough for you, then I think you are a Christian unbeliever, these Christian have to see with their eyes and hear with their ears before they can believe, so I called them Christian unbelievers. Just in case you are one of these Christian unbeliever, I recommend that you give Jesus a call, I am very sure he can help. Jesus told Thomas, blessed are they that have not seen, and yet have believed (John 20:29). After reading this book and you cannot see that dreams do reveals secrets and hidden things I recommend that you read the Bible some more, give it a shot it will make you wise.

## THE DREAM OF A LADY

Some years ago I heard a sister of the church who testify that one night she had a dream hearing the voice of a man telling her to feel one of her breast, I cannot remember which one, so the morning when she woke she examine her breast just as she was told in the dream, to her amazement she found a lump in her breast. So she went to the doctor and they took an xray and there it was (Cancer) but something wonderful happen, the cancer was dead, it could not spread any further so they took it out and she was fine. The Lord do talk to his people through dreams and visions today.

## MY DOCTOR AND I

Some years ago I heard the voice of a man telling me in a dream change your doctor, SO I never see that doctor any more. 4 or 5 years past, then I went to see another doctor, he took some blood test and I was a type 2 diabetic, I could not believe it, but it is true. But thank God it is under very good control. I believe if I had go and see another doctor earlier, they would catch it early and I would not have diabetes today. Doctors will tell you that to beat many disease is to treat it early. My advice is this, if you should dreams of this kind, Act today and not tomorrow because your health or your life could depend on that dream.

Job said, For God speaketh once, yea twice, yet man perceiveth it not. IN a dream, in a vision of the night, when deep sleep fallen upon men, in slumberings upon the bed, (Job 33:14-15). God is doing his part to inform us and to protect us but too many times we are slow of heart to believe and understand.

## A VISION OF DISCOURAGEMENT

*I*N september 2007, one night I had a dream that I was to take a very long journey to a place that I have never been to before and the only way to get there was to fly, but there was a young lady who wanted to go too but she could not fly so I had to fly with her on my back. It was a very long journey over a vast jungle, I was heading for a mansion in the middle of no where. Although I never been there before yet I know where I was going, but this young lady was a problem, when we fly for a while and she could not see where I was going she started to complain over and over again, she was asking me where is the place I said I was going, and she started to slide off my back over and over again, to one side and I keep telling her to stay straight on my back because you could fall.

I was flying at a very high speed so if she slide off in the jungle below there would be no hope for her then finally we saw this great mansion in a distant and she began to say thank you brother thank you very much, so I said to her you are telling me thanks because you can see it with your eyes. IF this young lady was somebody I know in real life I would sure to have a chat with her because she need some encouragement, her behaviour represent many.

The meaning of this dream has to do with the Christian

journey, the mansion in heaven our final destination but many are getting discourage along the way and are sliding back into the jungles of sin where there is no hope. All that sin have to offer is death, any one who choose death over life is in darkness. now the just shall live by faith: but if any man draw back, my soul shall have no pleasure in him, Rom 10:38). Remember dreams are illustrations or a picture of what is to come. God uses these illustrations as his language to inform us or forewarn us of what is coming because his ways and thoughts are higher than ours, (Isaiah 55:9

## WHAT WOULD JESUS DO

*R*eligious leaders are sitting in the seat that Jesus would have sit in if he was here in the flesh, but are they doing what Jesus would have done? IN Matt 23:1-3, we read, Then spake Jesus to the multitude, and to his disciples, saying, The scribes and the pharisees sit in Moses seat: All therefore whatsoever they bid you to observe, that observe and do; but do not ye after their works, for they say, and do not.

Obey the word of God even if it comes from hypocrites, but do not live like them. The works of hypocrites were done to be seen of others, and we have many of them today, they are saying many things that Jesus have said but they do not the things that Jesus would have done. Christians are given the power of attorney to act in Jesus place, to do the things that Jesus would have done. IF I should ask you, would Jesus use the sins that were committed ten years ago against us today, you would ask me if I am loosing my mind, you would quote me all the scripture in the Bible to let me know how he forgive our sins and remove them as far as the east is from the west and cast them into the sea of forgetfulness and he would remember them no more.

But there are some who claim to be acting on behalf of Jesus Christ and they are using the faults of others that happen many years before, what would Jesus do? These people said zero tolerance in their church for God's people, if God to say that, where would we stand? So these people are saying there will be no mercy or compassion for those that do wrong. That's not what the Bible teaches such are man made rules. Zero tolerance is not of God, Jesus TEACHES LOVE, MERCY, AND COMPASSION, Jesus said let the wheat and the tares grow together until the day of harvest, Matt 13:30).

Paul said, Take heed therefore unto yourselves, and to all the flock, over the which the Holy Ghost hath made you overseers, to feed the church of God, which he hath purchased with his own blood. For I know this, that after my departing shall grievous wolves enter in among you, not sparing the flock, (Acts 20:28-29).

Again Paul said, Brethren, if a man be overtaken in a fault, ye which are spiritual, restore such a person in the spirit of meekness; considering thyself, lest you also be tempted. Bear ye one another's burdens, and so fulfill the law of Christ, Gal 6:1-2) which is the law that do not condemned,. What hurting people need is somebody who cares, somebody who understand to lend them a helping hand, many people are battered by the storms of life, they cannot see clearly any more, perplexity take hold of them, may be problems in the marriage, financial problems, for heaven sake, these people need a friend, be that friend, a friend with a heart of compassion, you claim to represent Christ in the world, what would Jesus do?

In the eyes of God, LOVE, MERCY, AND COMPASSION worth for more than all man made church rules combined. Jesus said blessed are the merciful for they shall obtain mercy.

## THE PARABLE OF THE GOOD SAMARITAN, LUKE 10:

*W*hat does it mean to be a good neighbour? And Jesus answering said, A certain man went down from Jerusalem to Jericho, and fell among thieves, which stripped him of his raiment and wounded him, and departed, leaving him half dead. And by chance there came down a certain priest that way; and when he saw him, he passed by on the other side. And likewise a Levite, when he was at the place, came and looked on him, and pass by on the other side. But a certain Samaritan, as he journeyed, came where he was; and when he saw him, he had compassion on him. And went to him, and bounds up his wounds pouring in oil and wine, and set him on his own beast, and brought him to an inn, and took care of him.

## A PRIEST AND THE LEVITES

The law of Moses made a sharp distinction between the priests and ordinary Levites. The priests belong to Aaron's family; and the Levites belongs to the larger family of Levi.A priest was a Levite; but a Levite was not necessarily a priest. Priest's were consecrated Exod 29:1-37, Leviticus 8,) Levites were purified Num 8:5-22). Jesus gave us an illustration of how to be a good neighbour. The road from Jerusalem to Jericho was a steep descent, which was about 18 miles east. It was called the bloody way, and a very dangerous area of palestine because robbers infested the country. Note the four things done by thieves Jericho was a priestly city. At least 12 thousand priests lived there who would frequently pass that way to minister in the temple.

It was a city of palm trees (Deut'.34:3, Judges 1:16). It was about 18 miles from Jerusalem and six from Jordan. This is the extent of the help of religious people who are bound by forms and rituals, which cannot be broken even to save a life. The priest and the Levite did two things, they looked on the wounded man and pass by on the other side "under the pretense of avoiding the unclean and the impure. A merciful, compassionate and godly man would have saved the life or help a person regardless of church rules, it is not a sin to be merciful and compassionate. It is sad to say, but we have these same kind of people in the church today, they are acting just like the politicians, they will investigate you, just to find something to use use against you to crush you, they know not how to be merciful and compassionate.

Jesus showed us the superiority of the gospel over the law, teaching us to reject any religion of law that would neglect a deed of mercy. See Lev 22, Num 19) The Samaritans were hated by the Jews, but now the despised come to the rescue of the man, showing deeds of mercy and human compassion when the respected and religious class will not. It would be a shame to see Christians acting in this manner. Rejection by men naturally works kindness and compassion in the human soul. Note the ten acts of mercy showed to the man by his neighbour v33-35.

This defines the word "neighbour" and illustrates how to be a good neighbour. The two pence that the inn keeper received worth two days pay for a common labourer so he was well paid. v40. This is the point Jesus conveyed by this illustration. His teachings were always very clear that the point was never lost if one wanted to accept the truth. IN the case of Matt 13:11-15, the people heard, but they would not open their minds to believe and receive the truth. Jesus applied this to the Lawyer to further answer his question of what to do to inherit eternal life. This will be automatically be practiced by people who are born again and have eternal life abiding in them (I John 3:15-18, 1 Cor 13). Our neighbour can be any one who is in need and to whom we have the opportunity to help.

From my experience I know that many unbelievers do show compassion and kindness when needed, but to see the unbeliever responded where the Christian fail would be a shame. John said, But whoso hath this world's good, and seeth his brother in need, and shutteth up his bowels of compassion from him, how dwelleth the love of God in him? 1 John 3:17

## JESUS, THE SCRIBES, AND THE PHARISEES

$\mathcal{A}$nd the Scribes and pharisees brought unto him a woman taken in adultery; and when they had set her in the midst. They say unto Jesus, Master, this woman caught in the act of adultery, now the law of Moses commanded us, that such a person should be stoned, but what do you say? This they said, tempting him, that they might find a way to accused him. But Jesus stooped down and with his fingers he wrote on the ground as if he did not heard them. So when they continued asking him, he lifted up himself, and said unto them, He that is without sin among you, let him first cast a stone at her. And Jesus stooped down again and wrote on the ground. And they which heard it were convicted by their own conscience, so they walk one by one leaving her alone, Jesus ask her where are your accusers?

Hath any one condemn you, she said no one Lord. And Jesus said unto her, neither do I Condemn thee;go, and sin no more John 8: 3-11. IF Jesus had contradicted the law of moses Lev 20:10, that said, And the man that committeth adultery with another man's wife, even he that committeth adultery with his neighbour's wife, the adulterer and the adulteress shall surely be put to death. and Deut 22:22-24, IF a man be found lying with a woman married to an husband, then both of them shall die both the man that lay with the woman, and the woman: so shalt thou put away evil from Israel. v23, If a damsel that is a virgin be betrothed unto a husband (or promise to marry her) and a man find her in the city, and lie with her. v24, Then ye shall bring them both out unto the gate of the city, and ye shall stone them with stones that they die; the damsel, because she cried not, being in the city; and the man, because he hath humbled his neighbour's wife, So thou shalt put away evil from among you.

He would be condemned as a false prophet. IF he had condemned the woman to death He would be accused to the Romans as usurping authority, so He merely wrote on the ground as if he did not hear them. So when they continued to ask, He told them that whosoever is without sin let him first cast the stone. What Jesus wrote on the ground is not recorded. Jesus know who they were, that they were just as guilty of sin as the woman that they were about to stone to death.

Their hypocrisy was well known to Jesus and others that were standing there. Their own evil designs turn against them and expose them. They were guilty of the same sin but because they were not caught they believe they have the right to judge the guilty. We have the same sought of hypocrites all around us today in our churches-The apostle Paul said, Therefore thou art inexcusable, O man whosoever thou art that judgest: for when thou judgest another, thou condemnest thyself: for thou that judgest doest the same things Romans 2:v1).Conscience is a wonderful thing, it is the faculty that decides the lawfulness of our actions as to right and wrong (Romans 2:12-16).

The law of moses requires both the man and the woman that commit this sin to be put to death, but they did not brought the man, why not? it is not recorded. IF the woman alone was to be put to death it would not be a just execution. If we would pay attention to the things that Jesus teaches we would be better Christians instead of just talking about them.

## THE DAY THE SUN STAND STILL

Joshua 10: 12-14

Now after the death of Moses the servant of the Lord it came to pass, that the Lord spake unto Joshua the son of Nun, Moses minister, saying, Moses my servant is dead, now therefore arise go over this Jordan, you, and all this people, unto the land which I do give unto them, even to the children of Israel. Josh 1:1-2. How the Lord spoke to Joshua is not stated, but it could have been by an audible voice, in a dream, by a vision, a prophecy, by the urim and thummin (Num 27:21). or by some other means. This first communication with Joshua could not be considered a introduction to the whole book and a guarantee that the theocracy started by Moses would be continued with the nation and that divine instruction would be continued with Joshua as the new leader, even though it might not be a face to face communication every time (Num 12:8)

This was a real divine miracle v14, wherein the sun and the moon stand still or stop their influences on the earth. It is not the only miracle in connection with the sun. The earth was in total darkness for an indefinite period of time, but when God said let there be light there was light Gen 1:2-3, There was darkness in Egypt for three full days, Exod 10:21-23, The shadow of the sun went back ten degrees on the sun dial of Ahaz 2 Kings 20:11, ISA 38:8, The sun went down at noon and the earth was in darkness when Israel fell by Babylon AMOS 8:9, And there was darkness for three hours when Jesus was crucified Luke 23:44-45,

(PROPHECY) The sun will be darkened in the 6th seal Rev 6:12-17, the 4th trumpet Rev 8:12, the 5th trumpet REV 9:2, the 5th vial Rev 16:10, and at the 2nd advent of Christ and Armageddon ISA 13:10, Ezek 32:7, Joel 2:10, 31, CH 3:15, Matt 24:29-31). What is the purpose of miracles? The purpose of miracles was to cause all men every where to know that God is the only true and living God (Exod 6:7, CH 7:5,17, CH 8:10, 22, CH 9:14, 29, CH 10:2, CH 11:7, CH 14:4, 18, CH 16:6, 12, CH 29:46, CH 31:13, Deut 29:6) And many other times, it is clear that God has done things to prove to all men that He is God. IN Ezekiel alone the statement is found over 75 times, such as, they shall know that I am the Lord.

When Joshua became the leader of Israel after the death of Moses, the Lord told him there shall be no man will be able to stand before you all the days of thy life; as I Was with Moses so will I be with thee: I will not fail thee, nor forsake thee. Be strong and of good courage; for unto this people shalt thou divide for an inheritance the land, which I swore unto their fathers to give them.

Only be thou strong and very courageous", that thou mayest observe to do according to the law, which my servant Moses commanded thee: turn not from it to the right hand or to the left, that mayest prosper whithersoever thou goest Joshua 1:5-7. Joshua was a faithful servant of the Lord, he hold fast to the command of God, When Israel started walk contrary to the law of God, he told them as for me and my house we will serve the Lord. Joshua was no stranger to what God can do, he had seen many miracles, he saw what God did to pharaoh and the Egyptians, how God open the red sea and Israel walk through on dry ground, he saw how God send manner from heaven and feed them, and how God take them across the river Jordan into the promise land. Joshua was a man of great faith and confidence in the God of Israel.

## GIBEON WAS IN TROUBLE AND CALL ON JOSHUA FOR HELP

*N*ow it came to pass, When Adonizedec king of Jerusalem heard how Joshua had taken all, and had utterly destroyed it, and how he did the same thing to Jericho and her king, and how Gibeon had made peace with Israel and were among them. The men of Gibeon saw the writing on the wall, knowing that they could not fight with the God of Israel and win, so they make peace with Israel. Adonizedec king of Jerusalem was very fearful because Gibeon was a great city, as one of the royal cities, and because it was greater than all, and all the men thereof were mighty Josh 10:1-2).

Adonizedec king of Jerusalem send messages to all the kings of the Amorites five in total, saying come and help us, let us smite Gibeon because they make peace with Israel. They responded, it was a big mistake to choose to fight with Israel, but it gave Joshua the occasion for the next move (v5-15) The king of Jerusalem, the king of Hebron the king of Jarmuth, the king of Lachish, the king of Eglon, v5. JOSHUA responded to the call but no doubt Joshua inquired of the Lord before making this move, Because the Lord said unto Joshua, fear them not; for I have delivered them into thine hand; there shall not a man of them stand before thee. Joshua and all his men of war march all night and attacked the five kings south of palestine and the Lord gave Israel complete victory which put them in possession of all this part of the land in canaan v8-14)

The Lord discomfited the enemies so that Israel get a speedy victory and slay them v10) the Lord cast down great hailstones from heaven so that more died from the miraculous hail stones than from the sword of Israel vll They were fighting for three whole days and one night.

The fight was vicious, the sword of Israel was doing great damage, the hails were coming down with one weighing as much as 260 lbs, and enemies started to ran, Joshua knew victory was near, with God on his side his faith and courage was at its highest peak, but he need more time for total victory, he need a few more hours, the day was far spent, the sun was going down and the night was coming. It was over the valley that Joshua saw the moon coming up at the time the sun was setting over Gibeon, when Joshua commanded the sun to stand still on Gibeon; and thou moon in the valley of Ajalon, and the sun and the moon stayed where they were for about a whole day and did not go down until total victory was won.

And there was not a day like that before it or after it, that the Lord hearkened unto the voice of a man: for the Lord fought for Israel v12-14). This was the first time man commanded the solar system to stand still, and it obeyed. At other time, God hearkened to Hezekiah and turned the solar system backward 10 degrees (2 kings 20: 9-11, ISA 38:8).

## A VISION OF A RIPENED TOMATO GARDEN

It was in october 2007 1 had this dream of a very beautiful tomato garden, all the tomato's was cherry red and ready for harvest, the tomato vines were like grape vines and they were loaded and ready for the reapers. The meaning of this dream is in Matt 9:37-

38, Then saith Jesus unto his disciples, the harvest truly is plenteous, but the labourers are few. pray ye therefore the Lord of the harvest, that he will send forth labourers into his harvest. These tomato's were different sizes and shapes, there were large ones, medium size ones, small ones, and very small ones.

There were large round ones, large oval shape ones, medium size round and oval shape ones and small ones. These different sizes and shapes represent the different nations and races of people. IF you should have dreams of this kind the Lord is talking to you. The Lord could be letting you know that you are needed in the vineyard, so you need to pay attention. Remember dreams are illustrations of what is happening or that which is to come, some dreams will come to pass in a very short time, others you have to wait, The dreamer need to keep notes on their dreams because they carry very important messages some dreams warns of evil forces that is coming your way so you need to remember, I have them so I am giving you the facts.

## A DREAM THAT REVEALS HIDDEN DANGER ABOUT A MOTHER AND HER CHILDREN

IN the year 2007 1 had a dream about a lady and one of her children. I dream that she was living at an apartment building and she went down to the lobby to get her son coming home from school, I was entering the building from the outside, when I enter the lobby I saw her son playing with a very dangerous little animal in the lobby, his mother was there watching him playing with the little animal.

I don't think she did know how dangerous the little creature was because that little boy could get a very nasty bite. IN the dream I know the creature was too dangerous for a kid to be playing with. So I called her and told the dream that I had, and she said your dream is true, and she told me what it was but I cant say. Although she knew what the situation was, the dream let her know that it was dangerous.(This is the interpretation of the dream) This lady have her own home, so the apartment building represent her own home, and that dangerous little animal was a real person living at her home, and she told me more than once how true my dream was.

IF the Lord don't reveal these things we will not know how serious some things are until its too late. This dream let her know that, that person could be a danger to her children. A dream can make us much more knowledgeable in regard to the things we have to deal with. IF you can see danger before they strike, I would say you are one step ahead of the devil and his plans if you take action to avoid them. It is not enough to know and do nothing, you must take action and that's how the battle is won.

## A HIGH SPEED TRAIN COMING TO CANADA

This is a vision of prophecy. It was in the year 2004 in a night vision the lord showed me a newly laid high speed train line. So when I woke from the dream I know that a high speed train will be coming to Canada so wait for it, it is coming. IN January 2008 1 heard a conversation on tv that canada need a high speed train.

## A DREAM OF ANIMALS FIGHTING ON A CHURCH PROPERTY

Some dreams are dreams of caution, the Lord reveal these things to put us on our guard so we can avoid certain situations, it was January 2008 1 had this dream, I dream seeing a donkey tied on a church property and two dogs attacking and biting the donkey until the donkey was bleeding, but the donkey fought back and bite the dogs too until they bleed too. What does it mean to see animals fighting on a church property? The animals represent the members of the church. Paul said, But if ye bite and devour one another, take heed that ye be not consumed one of another Gal 5:15). IF you should have a dream of this kind you must be on your watch.

## DID YOU KNOW THAT GOD ASK QUESTIONS?

(ATTENTION PLEASE) PSALM 1, and PSALM 14, is not my idea to put them in the book, it is the Lord's. After I started to write the book and reach some where between 80 and 90 pages, then in a night vision the Lord ask me a question, I heard these words, have you considered PSALM 1 and PSALM 14? 1 did not think about putting them in the book but the Lord want them in the book. For you who do not understand that God talk to people today, I want you to know that this is his portion He put in the book confirming to me that his words are true and that He is with me in writing this book-The Lord is still working with us when we are doing things for his glory and honor.-

## OIL

To dream that you are being showered or sprayed with oil is a very good dream, it mean that something pleasant is coming your way.

TO Dream that you see pure beautiful oil flowing from out of the ground, represent prosperity.

## A MAJOR RELIGIOUS ORGANIZATION IS DENOUNCED BY GOD

ATTENTION PLEASE, In 1965 1 was a young Christian in my home church, I always listen to preachers on the radio, I did not know who they were but I know they were ministers of the gospel of Christ. Then one night in a night vision the Lord pointed out two of these preachers to me so I could know who they were. I heard these words, Oral Robert and Billy Graham is under the power of God, He was not ashamed to be called their God and he let me know it. I did not have to wonder any more who they were because the Lord told me.

IF the Lord should tell you of others that they are not his, and that they are not a Christian religion would you believe him? I will let you answer the question. The Bible teaches that the Lord knoweth them that are his. And, let every one that nameth the name of christ depart from iniquity 2 TIM 2:19).IF the Lord should tell you that you are not a Christian and you don't believe him your arguments would be useless, there would be only one way out and that is total repentance.

In the month of April 2008 1 was in a night vision talking with a lady about church and religion and it was told that a certain religious organization in our world is not a Christian religion, I am sorry I cannot tell you the name of the church. If you believe what I said about Oral Robert and Billy Graham believe this one also because it is the same God who reveal them both. while the lady and myself was talking about this church there was a young man standing near by but he was not in conversation but he was listening to what we were saying and when he heard that this church was not a Christian religion he said thank you Jesus, he was very surprise because he did not know.

PLEASE NOTE, This young man represent many who do not know that this is not a Christian religion. I can tell you that this is a very old church, and that it did much harm to the early Christians. It is a very large church with millions of members. It was also revealed that if one want to know the truth about this church they should go back to their history. The Lord want you to know that it is not a Christian religion.

## A VISION OF THE SOUL OF MAN

The flesh is not the real you, your soul is the real you, the flesh is temporary, the soul is eternal, the soul will live forever either in heaven or in hell, as long as God lives your soul lives. IF you should see your soul would it make you a better Christian? IF YOU should see the other you would you take better care of him or her so that the soul would not perish, the soul is the other you looking just like you with the same size, same height, same color, same color hair, same color eyes, there is no difference between you now and your soul.

For one to save the soul depend on the right choice, to reject Christ you damn the soul, to accept Christ you save the soul, in 1 John 5: 11-12, we read, And this is the record, that God hath given us eternal life, and this life is in his son. v12, He that hath the son hath life; and he that hath not the son of God hath not life. Too much attention is given to the flesh over the soul by some Christians, they don't care what the Bible have say they just choose to please themselves and not God, they love this present world and what it have to offer and that is dangerous for the soul. There are too many Christians who still do not get it that the soul is a real person just as they are real in the flesh but cannot be release until at the time of death.

The apostle Paul said, We are confident, I say, and willing rather to be absent from the body, and to be present with the Lord 2 Cor 5:8). It is sown a natural body, it is raised a spiritual body, There is a natural body, and there is a spiritual body 1 Cor 15: 44. The flesh has no value it is from the dust of the earth and to dust it shall return, but with the soul it is a different matter, it is priceless, so Jesus ask the question, For what shall it profit a man, if he shall gain the whole world, and lose his own soul? or what shall a man give in exchange for his soul? Mark 8:36-37). Can you answer the question? the answer is christ himself nothing else will do.

I am not the only one who saw the soul of man, ON the mount of transfiguration, Peter, James,and John was with Jesus and they saw the souls of Moses and Elias talking with Jesus Matt 17:1-3).IN Revelation 6:9-11, John said, And when he had opened the fifth seal, I saw under the altar the souls of them that were slain for the word of God, and for the testimony which they held; And they cried with a loud, voice, saying, How long, o Lord, holy and true, dost thou not judge and avenge our blood on them that dwell on the earth?

vll, And white robes were given unto every one of them; and it was said unto them, that they should rest yet for a little season, until their fellow servants also their brethren, that should be killed as they were, should be fulfilled. Having seen this vision about the soul of man I realize the Lord was reinforcing what the Bible already said about the matter. ATTENTION PLEASE, Some years ago I was in a night vision and the Lord showed me myself as three of us, .the Lord was talking to me which is my spirit, the Lord was telling me about what is going to happen to the other two of me that was standing a little way off which is my soul and my body. So man is made up of spirit, soul, and a body just as the Bible teaches, I saw all three of them. We were exactly the same, we were just like identical twin and I heard the voice of the Lord said unto me, one of you will live to a certain age of which I know how long I will live and the other one he said there will be no end to your life, this is the physical body and the soul, we cannot see the soul or-the spirit only a revelation from the Lord can reveal them to us, I have this revelation.

(Listen to this) I was not in the habit of keeping notes of my dreams so as the years goes by I forget how long I will live, I just could not remember but two numbers stuck in my head, I know it was one of them but I still could not remember which was the right one and this goes on for about 2 or 3 years, the Lord know I forget and suddenly one night in a vision the Lord spoke to me again and told me how long I will live for the second time and it was one of those numbers that stuck in my head, the Lord is like a father who love his children, and even more.

IN Luke 16: 19-31 Jesus gave us a clear picture of the immortality of the soul and the consciousness of the soul after it leave the body, Jesus make it very clear that the soul of the righteous will go to a place of bliss and the soul of the wicked will go to a place of torment or hell Jesus make it very clear what the soul of man look like. This was an actual experience of two men, not a parable, Jesus said, There was a certain rich man which was clothed in purple and fine linen, and fared sumptuously every day, or he dress lavishly every day. v20,And there was a certain beggar named Lazarus, which was laid at his gate, full of sores. v2l, And desiring to be fed with the crumbs which fell from the rich man's table, and dogs came and licked his sores.

Jesus said the beggar died, and was carried by angels into Abraham's bosom: the rich man also died and was buried. Jesus said the rich man went to hell and lift up his eyes, being in torments, and seeth Abraham afar off and Lazarus in his bosom, meaning he was close to Abraham being comforted. Jesus said the rich man cried to father Abraham to have mercy on him, and begged Abraham to send Lazarus with a little water on the tip of his finger to cool his tongue because he was in a flame being tormented.

v25, But Abraham said, son, remember when you were alive you have all the good things, and likewise Lazarus the evil things: but now he is comforted, and thou art tormented.

These are the same two men who know each other in their life time and even after death they remain exactly the same persons. If you cannot see from this story that you and your soul is identical to you then you are sleeping and need to be awaken. The apostle Paul said, Wherefore we labour, that, whether present or absent, we may be accepted of him. For we must all appear before the judgment seat of christ; that every one may receive the things done in his body, according to that he hath done, whether it be good or bad 2 Cor 5:9-10). It is clear that what we do now in the flesh we will give an account to God in the next life after we die.

IN this life people get themselves lawyers to plead their case with their smart arguments to outsmart the court of law, but on that day when we stand before the eternal judge there is no one that will be able to outsmart him, Jesus made it very clear that the way we live determine our destiny.

If there is any one who knows about the soul of man it is Jesus the son of God because he was with the father when God said, Let us make man in our image, and after our likeness ... So God created man in his own image, in the image of God created he him; male and female created he them. Gen 1:26-27). And the Lord God formed man of-the dust of the ground, and breathed into his nostrils the breath of life; and man became a living soul. CH 2:v7. John said, All things were made by him: and without him was not any thing made that was made. John 1:v3).

Your soul is you, the English word man "occures in the Bible over 3000 times, ln Heb, and Gr, in many cases the meaning is different but at end it mean that man is a soul with a body. Paul-said, For I delight in the law of God after the inward man. (Rom 7:22). Man also has a spirit (Cor 2:11),the moral nature which makes man religious, and gives him a conscience- It is truly a privilege the Lord has given to me to have a look at the soul of man and to know what we will look like in the other life. I do not believe the Lord gave me this revelation to throw it into the trash can and no one knows about it, the Lord wants to encourage and comfort one another as we see the day approaching.

Paul said, Be not deceived; God is not mocked for whatsoever a man soweth, that shall he also reap. For he that soweth to his flesh shall of the flesh reap corruption; but he that soweth to the spirit shall of the spirit reap life everlasting. (Gal 6:7-8). Just as everything in nature produces after its kind so it is for you and I, you are encourage to sow to the spirit and reap eternal life.

### VANITY OF VANITIES

ALL IS VANITY. ECCL 1:v2

What is vanity? it means emptiness, evanescence, worthlessness, futility, and is applied to things that are empty or worthless, such as fruitlessness of human endeavors, it appears 37 times in the Book of Ecclesiastes alone. Man's natural life is vanity, Job 7:v3, PSALMS 39:5-6, etc).King Solomon son of king David is the world wisest man ever lived, but Solomon had a problem, he loved many strange women together with the daughter of pharaoh, woman of the moabites, the Ammonites, Edomites, the Zidonians, and the Hittites. These are the very nations that the Lord told the children of Israel, ye shall not go in to them, neither shall they come in unto you: for surely they will turn away your heart after their gods: but Solomon clave unto these women in love.

And he had seven hundred wives, princesses, and three hundred concubines and his wives turned his heart from the Lord. The more he clave to these strange women, the more his heart grow cold toward God. They finally turned his heart away from the Lord entirely, and his heart became imperfect before God in love and service, 1 kings 11,1-4). Solomon became king when he was about twenty years old and reigned over Jerusalem and all Israel for about forty years and died at age sixty v42. He lost his first love for the Lord, but he leave a great lesson for us that the pleasures of this world and sin is vanity, they carry no value.

IT IS ALL VANITY) David said, Behold, thou hast made my days as an handbreath; and mine age is as nothing before thee: verily every man at his best state is all together vanity. Surely every man walketh in a vain shew: surely they are disquieted in vain: he heapeth up riches, and knoweth not who shall gather them, PSALMS 39:5-6).A little that a righteous man hath is better than the riches of many wicked. For the arms of the wicked shall be broken: but the Lord upholdeth the righteous. The Lord knoweth the days of the upright: and their inheritance shall be for ever, PSALM 37:16-18

This is always true due to the blessing of the Lord upon the little. A righteous man is contented with little under the most trying circumstances when it is blessed by his heavenly father. Solomon said, better is little with the fear of the Lord than great treasure and trouble therewith. Better is a dinner of herbs where love is, than a stalled ox and hatred there with, prov 15:16-17, 1 Cor 10:31,1 thess 5:18, IN every thing give thanks.

## ITS ALL VANITY, MAN'S WORKS IS UNPROFITABLE

$\mathcal{L}$ets learn from the wisest man ever lived, King Solomon, son of King David. What profit hath a man of all his labour which he taketh under the sun? one generation passeth away, and another generation cometh: but the earth abideth for ever, ECCL 1:3-4. Life in the present society is based upon profit and loss. The profit,for the most part, according to Solomon in this book, is nothing but to eat and drink, and be merry, and fulfill the lust of the heart, ECCL 2:1-3. 1 have seen all the works that are done under the sun, and, and behold all is vanity and vexation of spirit. The true program of righteousness is that a man should work to support his own house (1 tim 5: v8) and help others Luke 6:38, Col 1:v10, 1 thess 4:11, and many more scripture, and share in the spreading of the gospel of Christ to the ends of the earth (Matt 28:19-20, Mark 16:15-20, Luke 24:47-51, Acts 1: 4-8

Ladies and gentlemen the only thing that carry any lasting value from man's work is that which is done for God and Christ because you are storing up treasures in heaven, the rest is vanity and vexation of spirit. Jesus said, Lay not up for yourselves treasures upon earth, where moth and rust doth corrupt, nd where thieves break through and steal. But lay up for yourselves treasures in heaven, where neither moth nor rust doth corrupt, and where thieves do not break through nor steal. For where your treasure is, there will your heart be also, Matt 6:19-21).

## PERSONAL PLEASURE IS VANITY IT LEAVES YOU EMPTY

$\mathcal{S}$olomon gave his heart to every pleasure that his heart lusted after and found that it was all vanity, he gave himself to wine, and acquainting his heart with wisdom: and to lay hold on folly, to see what was good for the sons of men, which they should do under the heaven all the days of their life. Solomon made great works: he builded himself houses, and planted vineyards: He made gardens

✧ ✧ ✧ ✧ ✧ ✧ ✧ ✧ ✧ ✧ ✧ ✧ ✧ ✧ ✧ ✧ ✧

and orchards, he plant trees in them of all kind of fruits: He made pools of water to water the trees that bringeth forth wood, and it was all vanity, Ecci 2:1-6). NO one whose heart is right with God will give himself to wine and abandon the will of God for his life and to lay hold on folly as Solomon did (v3).

NO Godly person would do it for an experiment, knowing it is contrary to the will of God for their lives. It seems that Solomon wanted to see if his wisdom would remain in his heart during a period of giving it over to sin. He found that his wisdom did remain: and such was the reason why he did it: that wisdom and knowledge become a part of the human mentality whether acquired by study, experience, divine revelation, or imparted by the Holy Spirit (v9).

## RICHES IS VANITY AND VAIN GLORY

Solomon had men servants and lady servants, he had servants born in his house: he also had great possessions of great and small cattle above all that were in Jerusalem before him, he had herds and flocks. He had silver and gold, and peculiar treasures of kings and the provinces, he had many men singers, and many women singers, Solomon had musical instruments of all kinds. Solomon did not lost his wisdom and knowledge which was given to him as gifts through the Holy Spirit, CH 2:7-9

## ALL IS VANITY

Solomon did not kept back from any thing, what ever his eyes desired he obtained, he rejoiced in his labour for that was his portion, He looked on all the works of his hands and found that all was vanity and vexation of spirit because there was no profit under the sun (vIO-11). VANITY: WISDOM AND FOLLY, Solomon said, I turned myself to behold wisdom, and madness, and folly: I have done it all. Then I saw that wisdom excelleth folly, as far as light excelleth darkness.

Solomon said, The wise man eyes are in his head: but the fool walketh in darkness: and I myself perceived also that one event happenth to them all. Then I said in my heart,as it happenth to the fool, so it happenth to me: and why was I then more wise? Then I said in my heart, that this is also vanity. Solomon said, there will be no remembrance of the wise more than the fool for ever, Solomon ask, And how dieth the wise man? as a fool, v16). Since Solomon conclude that all earthly wisdom and knowledge is vanity, then where are the wise? they can only be found in the Lord Jesus Christ because the wisdom of this world is foolishness where God is concern, Solomon said, The fruit of the righteous is a tree of life; and he that winneth soul is wise. The righteous produce eternal life for men by winning them to Christ, prov 11:30) Both the righteous and the wicked will reap what they sow v3l; Gal 6:7-8).

Solomon discovered that there is no supreme good or lasting happiness in all the pursuits of science, that there is no genuine satisfaction in unbridled lust, that there is no true joy to folly, and that wisdom excels folly as much as light reign supreme over darkness ECCL 2:(v13) The wise man eyes are in his head, meaning that he weighs carefully the consequences of all that he does, but the fool has no guide to his reasons and no check on his passions because his lustful heart keep him blind(v14). Ladies and gentlemen both the wise man and the fool dies, they share the same fate, if you seek to be wise let it be towards God by doing so you will truly be wise. James said, If any of you lack wisdom, let him ask of God, that giveth to all men liberally, and upbraideth not: and it shall be given him, JAMES 1:v5

Solomon said, Let us hear the conclusion of the whole matter: Fear God, and keep his commandments, for this is the whole duty of man. For God shall bring every work into Judgment, with every secret thing, whether it be good, or whether it be evil, ECCL 12: 13-14).

Being wise towards God pays very high dividend, Isaiah

✧ ✧ ✧ ✧ ✧ ✧ ✧ ✧ ✧ ✧ ✧ ✧ ✧ ✧ ✧ ✧ ✧

the prophet said, And the ransomed of the Lord shall return, and come to Zion with songs and everlasting joy upon their heads: they shall obtain joy and gladness,and sorrow and sighing shall flee away, (ISAIAH 33:10). It will be joy, joy forever upon the crystal shore when all the saints shall gather to hear well done.

## A DREAM THAT IS NOT PLEASANT, WHAT COULD THIS MEAN?

$\mathcal{I}$ dream of a unpleasant situation two times in one night, so when I woke that morning I was lying on my back trying to make sense of it all and I heard a voice said, a uncontrolled demon this is a divine interpretation so if you should have this dream two times in one night mean you are dealing with a uncontrolled demon, so you must identify this demon and deal with it. The same is true if you have a pleasant dream, it mean things are going well for you so please give much attention to your dreams because they are talking to you.

## A VISION OF PROPHECY ABOUT THE UNITED STATES OF AMERICA

$\mathcal{O}$N August 24/2008 1 came home from church that sunday night and went to bed, and I heard these words in a vision of the night., BARAK OBAMA president of America will lead the polls about 100,000 a week which mean he would win for sure, you will see this prophecy come to pass before your very eyes which mean that God ruleth in the kingdom of men and that He will set up whosoever He choose. For the people who do not believe that there are prophets in the church today please read EPH 4:vll, And he gave some apostles, and some, prophets, and some, evangelists and some pasters and teachers.

# CONCLUSION

Dreams and visions are true but the understanding of many are lacking, there are some religious leaders who do not believe in dreams and are teaching God's people not to believe in dreams, they are using their head knowledge and plant doubts in the hearts of God's people, these people are in serious error and should not be believed. God and his words will always be true and every man a liar. These people are quick to point out that it is the devil or something else that is doing it, that mean God is not talking to his people only the devil or something else. It makes no different to me if they are deans, bishop, or pastors, if they speak against the word of God they are in serious error.

The word of God teaches that we will dream dreams and see visions Joel 2:28-29, Acts 18:9-1l, and many more scripture that speak about dreams and visions we cannot choose from God's word what we like and through the rest in the trash basket, such privilege is not given to the Christian church. Dreams are much more than just a dream, they encourage the dreamer, the dreamer see things in a different light, they creates alertness, the dreamer is very aware of what to expect, they put us on our guard. IF there were no benefit in dreams for the Christians why would the Lord tell us that we are going to have them?.

For one to conclude and to say that all that the Lord have to say He have already said it in the scripture and He have nothing more to say, such a person is very shallow spiritually and have not that spiritual depth of understanding the revelation of the Lord. I said this before and I am saying again that many years ago the Lord told me in a dream how long I will live and how I will die. I also said that I heard the voice of an angel of the Lord in a dream who said to me, the Lord said to tell you your sins are forgiven.

❖  ❖  ❖  ❖  ❖  ❖  ❖  ❖  ❖  ❖  ❖  ❖  ❖  ❖  ❖  ❖

These are the kind of benefit one can expect from a dream. IF this is not God then who is it? I will let you answer the question.

We read in the Bible from Genesis to revelation how God reveal himself to people in a dream or a vision, we read about them, we talk about them, we preach about them, if you and I don't talk about what the Lord is doing today, who will?. The word of the Lord remain the same today, if He said so then there is no power in hell to change it-If these are not enough for you to understand that God talk to people today then your spiritual understanding is impaired If you have problems with dreams the word of God tell us how to deal with this situation, see Deut 13:1-3, Jer 23:25-32, 1 John 4:1-6 and more.

# CONTENTS